WHAT A WORLD 1
LISTENING

Amazing Stories
from Around the Globe

Milada Broukal

☆ Vocabulary unit 3 - 9 - 10 - 12
☆ Pronunciation final "s" "ed"
- question intonation ↑↓
- word stress
☆ listening

PEARSON
Longman

What a World Listening 1: Amazing Stories from Around the Globe

Pearson Education, 10 Bank Street, White Plains, NY 10606 USA

Staff credits: The people who made up the *What a World Listening 1* team, representing editorial, production, design, and manufacturing, are Pietro Alongi, Rhea Banker, John Brezinsky, Aerin Csigay, Gina DiLillo, Nancy Flaggman, Oliva Fernandez, Lisa Ghiozzi, Emily Lippincott, Amy McCormick, Linda Moser, Jennifer Stem, and Patricia Wosczyk.
Cover and text design: Patricia Wosczyk
Text composition: ElectraGraphics, Inc.
Text font: Minion
Photo Credits: Cover, Thanachai Wachiraworakam/Flickr RF/Getty Images; Page 1, Joseph Reid/Alamy; p. 4, (left) Shutterstock.com, (right) Fotolia.com; p. 8, Hinata Haga/HAGA/The Image Work; p. 11, (left) Shutterstock.com, (right) Shutterstock.com; p. 15, Shutterstock.com; p. 18, (left) Shutterstock.com, (right) Shutterstock.com; p. 22, Louise Batalla Duran/Alamy; p. 25, (left) Shutterstock.com, (right) Shutterstock.com; p. 29, Shutterstock.com; p. 32, (left) Shutterstock.com, (right) Shutterstock.com; p. 36, Shutterstock.com; p. 39, (left) Shutterstock.com, (right) Shutterstock.com; p. 43, Fotolia.com; p. 46, (left) iStockphoto.com, (right) Juniors Bildarchiv/Alamy; p. 50, Blickwinkel/Alamy; p. 53, (left) Shutterstock.com, (right) Shutterstock.com, p. 57, Shutterstock.com; p. 60, (left) Shutterstock.com, (right) Shutterstock.com; p. 64, Shutterstock.com; p. 67, (left) Bryan Allen/Corbis, (right) Shutterstock.com; p. 75, AP Images/James Nachtwey; p. 78, (left) Bettmann/Corbis, (right) SuperStock RM/Getty Images; p. 82, Shutterstock.com; p. 85, (left) EmmePi Images/Alamy, (right) Shutterstock.com; p. 89, Shutterstock.com; p. 92, (left) Shutterstock.com, (right) Shutterstock.com; p. 96, Shutterstock.com; p. 99, (left) Shutterstock.com, (right) iStockphoto.com; p. 103, Shutterstock.com; p. 106, (left) Dreamstime.com, (right) Science Faction/SuperStock; p. 110, Shutterstock.com; p. 113, (left) Shutterstock.com, (right) Shutterstock.com; p. 117, BL Images Ltd/Alamy; p. 120, (left) Shutterstock.com, (right) Shutterstock.com; p. 124, Shutterstock.com; p. 127, (left) Shutterstock.com, (right) Shutterstock.com; p. 131, Shutterstock.com; p. 134, (left) Shutterstock.com, (right) Dreamstime.com; p. 138, Tim Graham/Alamy; p. 141, (left) Allstar Picture Library/Alamy, (right) AP Images/Associated Press

Library of Congress Cataloging-in-Publication Data

Broukal, Milada.
  What a world listening : amazing stories from around the globe / Milada Broukal.
    p. cm.—(What a world listening : amazing stories from around the globe series)
  Previously published as: What a world, 2004.
  ISBN 0-13-247389-5 (v. 1)—ISBN 0-13-247795-5 (v. 2)—ISBN 0-13-138200-4 (v. 3)
1. English language—Textbooks for foreign speakers. 2. Listening. I. Title.
  PE1128.B717 2010
  428.2'4—dc21

                                                                                                2010037494

ISBN-13: 978-0-13-247389-7
ISBN-10: 0-13-247389-5

PEARSON LONGMAN ON THE WEB

Pearsonlongman.com offers online resources for teachers and students. Access our Companion Websites, our online catalog, and our local offices around the world.

Visit us at **www.pearsonlongman.com**.

Printed in the United States of America
2 3 4 5 6 7 8 9 10–V011–15 14 13 12 11

CONTENTS

UNIT	VOCABULARY	LANGUAGE FOCUS	PRONUNCIATION
1 WHAT ARE SOME POPULAR KINDS OF BOOKS? PAGES **1–7**	*download • eBook • fiction • hardcover • nonfiction • novels • paperback • series* *comic books • make time • video games*	to have	*-teen* and *-ty*
2 WHAT DO YOU KNOW ABOUT NEW YEAR'S GREETINGS? PAGES **8–14**	*bundle • electronics • mailboxes • postcards • prepaid • presents • separate • temporary* *lottery numbers • New Year's Day • postal service*	Present Progressive	*th* and *t*
3 WHAT DO YOU KNOW ABOUT FAMOUS PALACES? PAGES **15–21**	*collection • drapes • elevators • flags • lawns • oval • rug • staircases* *free of charge • gives a speech • take a tour*	Simple Present	Third Person *-s*
4 WHAT ANIMALS ARE USEFUL TO HUMANS? PAGES **22–28**	*ashes • fertilizer • fuel • produce • sacred • survive • tractors • utensils* *depend on • family member • plow the field*	Simple Present with Adverbs of Frequency	Reduced Form of *do* and *does*
5 WHAT DO YOU KNOW ABOUT GIFT GIVING? PAGES **29–35**	*appropriate • beliefs • host • modesty • occasions • respect • suitable • symbolizes* *gift giving • give up • make a suggestion*	Comparative Adjectives	*-er*
6 WHAT ARE SOME TYPICAL FOODS FROM AROUND THE WORLD? PAGES **36–42**	*cabbage • cucumbers • radishes • recipe • region • sour • spicy • tastes* *in season • modern times • to get together*	Count and Non-count Nouns	Reduced Form of *and*

INTRODUCTION

What a World: Amazing Stories from Around the Globe—the series

This series now has two strands: a listening strand and a reading strand. Both strands explore linked topics from around the world and across history. They can be used separately or together for maximum exploration of content and development of essential listening and reading skills.

	Listening Strand	Reading Strand
Level 1 (Beginning)	*What a World Listening 1*	*What a World Reading 1, 2e*
Level 2 (High-Beginning)	*What a World Listening 2*	*What a Word Reading 2, 2e*
Level 3 (Intermediate)	*What a World Listening 3*	*What a Word Reading 3, 2e*

What a World Listening 1—a beginning listening and speaking skills book

It is the first in a three-book series of listening and speaking skills for English language learners. The twenty units in this book correspond thematically with the units in *What a World Reading 1, 2e*. Each topic is about different people, plants, animals, places, customs, or objects. The topics span history and the globe, from Australia, to national emblems, to the ancient Greeks.

Unit Structure and Approach

BEFORE YOU LISTEN opens with a picture of one of the people, plants, animals, places, customs, or objects featured in the unit. Prelistening questions follow. Their purpose is to motivate students to listen, encourage predictions about the content of the listening, and involve the students' own experiences when possible. Vocabulary can be presented as the need arises.

LONG TALK can be any one of a variety of scenarios, including a class lecture, a long conversation between two people, or a tour guide speaking to a group. The talk is generally about 250–300 words long. After an initial listening for general content, the teacher may wish to explain the words in the vocabulary section. The students should then do a second, closer listening, perhaps in chunks. Further listening can be done depending on the students' requirements.

VOCABULARY exercises focus on the important topic-related words in the long talk. Both *Meaning* and *Words that Go Together* are definition exercises that encourage students to work out the meanings of words from the context. *Meaning* focuses on single words. *Words that Go Together* focuses on collocations or groups of words which are easier to learn together the way they are used in the language. The third exercise, *Use*, reinforces the vocabulary further by making students use the words or collocations in a meaningful, yet possibly different, context. This section can be done during or after the listening to the long talk, or both.

COMPREHENSION exercises appear in each unit and consist of *Understanding the Listening* and *Remembering Details.* These confirm the content of the talk either in general or in detail. These exercises for developing listening skills can be done individually, in pairs, in small groups, or as a class. It is preferable to do these exercises in conjunction with the long talk, since they are not meant to test memory.

TAKING NOTES is a fun feature where students listen to a short description of a person, place, or thing related to the unit. It is not necessary for students to understand every word, but they are encouraged to take notes. From their notes, they decide which of the two options they are given fits the description.

SHORT CONVERSATIONS consists of three new conversations related to the topic of the unit. The exercises focus on content as well as the speaker's tone and attitude, what the speaker is doing, the speaker's job, and where the conversation is taking place.

DISCUSSION questions encourage students to bring their own ideas to the related topics in each long talk. They can also provide insights into cultural similarities and differences.

CRITICAL THINKING questions give students the opportunity to develop thinking skills (comparing and contrasting cultural customs, recognizing personal attitudes and values, etc.).

LANGUAGE FOCUS draws on a grammatical structure from the listening and offers exercises to help students develop accuracy in speaking and writing. The exercises build from controlled to more open-ended.

PRONUNCIATION exercises focus on a recurring pronunciation feature in the unit. These exercises help students to hear and practice word endings, reductions, stress, and intonation.

CONVERSATION exercises start with a set conversation for students to listen to and repeat. Then students progress to a freer conversation that they create using expressions from the set conversations.

Additional Activities

INTERNET ACTIVITIES (in the Appendices) help students develop their Internet research skills. Each activity can be done in a classroom setting or, if the students have Internet access, as homework leading to a presentation or discussion in class. There is an Internet activity for each unit and it is always related to the theme of the unit. It helps students evaluate websites for their reliability and gets them to process and put together the information in an organized way.

SELF-TESTS after Unit 10 and Unit 20 review general listening comprehension, vocabulary, and grammar in a multiple-choice format.

✳ ✳ ✳ ✳ ✳

The **Answer Key** for *What a World Listening 1* is available at the following website: http://www.pearsonlongman.com/whataworld.

WHAT ARE SOME POPULAR KINDS OF BOOKS?

before you listen

Answer these questions.

1. What kinds of books do you like?
2. What is your favorite book?
3. When and where do you like to read?

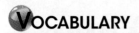

MEANING

🎧 *Listen to the talk. Then write the correct words in the blanks.*

download	fiction	nonfiction	paperback
eBook	hardcover	novels	series

1. Romance _____ are stories about love or adventure.

2. My _____ is a light book with a soft cover.

3. I have all the books in the _____ about the Old West.

4. This book is _____. It is about people and events that are not true or real.

5. I am reading a _____ book about the life of a young girl in the 1920s.

6. Most of my schoolbooks are _____ books. They are large and heavy.

7. I _____ information from websites to my personal computer.

8. I get books for my _____ reader from websites.

WORDS THAT GO TOGETHER

Write the correct words in the blanks.

comic books	make time	video games

1. My little brother plays _____ on his computer every night.

2. I like stories with pictures, so I have many _____.

3. It is important to _____ to do the things you love.

USE

Work with a partner to answer the questions. Use complete sentences.

1. What is one kind of *nonfiction* book?

2. What kinds of *novels* do you like to read?

3. What is nice about *paperback* books?

4. Do you play *video games*? Why or why not?

5. What are some popular *comic books* that people like?

6. Why are most schoolbooks *hardcover* books?

7. What would you like to *make time* to do?

8. What do you *download* most often?

COMPREHENSION: LONG TALK

UNDERSTANDING THE LISTENING

Listen to the talk. Then circle the letter of the correct answer.

1. Why is Ben's backpack so heavy?

   a. He has an eBook reader in there.
   b. He has his science books in there.
   c. He has paperback books in there.

2. Why does Yumi like her eBook reader?

   a. It has all the Harry Potter books on it.
   b. It is light.
   c. It is just like a hardcover book.

3. Which is true about Yumi?

   a. She likes to read all the time.
   b. She uses hardcover books for her classes.
   c. She likes to play video games.

REMEMBERING DETAILS

*Listen to the talk again. Circle **T** if the sentence is true. Circle **F** if the sentence is false.*

1.	Ben has paperback books in his backpack.	T	F
2.	Yumi thinks eBook readers are big and heavy.	T	F
3.	Ben likes to read.	T	F
4.	Ben likes fiction better than nonfiction.	T	F
5.	Yumi likes to make time to read.	T	F
6.	Ben is not into video games.	T	F

TAKING NOTES: Kinds of Books

🎧 *Listen and write notes about the description. Which book does it describe?*

hardcover book

eBook

COMPREHENSION: SHORT CONVERSATIONS

🎧 *Listen to the conversations. Then circle the letter of the correct answer.*

CONVERSATION 1

1. Who is the woman?

   a. a teacher
   b. a clerk in the bookstore
   c. a student

CONVERSATION 2

2. What kind of book does the man have to read on the airplane?

   a. nonfiction
   b. fiction
   c. romance

CONVERSATION 3

3. Why is the woman unhappy?

   a. The man doesn't have any books to give her.
   b. The bookstore doesn't have all the books in the series.
   c. She doesn't have enough money for all the books in the series.

DISCUSSION

Discuss the answers to these questions with your classmates.

1. Do you like fiction or nonfiction books? Why?
2. Do you carry heavy books for your classes? What kinds of books do you prefer: hardcover books, paperback books, or eBooks? Why?
3. Do you read comic books? Why or why not? Which ones do you read? Why are comic books not only for children?

CRITICAL THINKING

Work with a partner. Ask each other the following questions. Discuss your answers.

1. Do you have an eBook reader? Why or why not? What are some good things about eBooks? What are some bad things? Are there good things about paperback books, too? Which do you like better, eBooks or paperback books? Why? Do you think eBooks are the only books for the future? Why or why not?

2. Some people say that nobody reads anymore. Do you agree? Why or why not? What stops people from reading in today's world? Do you think it is important for people to read? Why or why not?

LANGUAGE FOCUS

TO HAVE

Statements	Questions and Answers
I/You/We/They **have** a book. I/You/We/They **don't (do not) have** a book.	**Q: Do** I/you/we/they **have** a book? **A: Yes,** I/you/we/they **do.** **No,** I/you/we/they **don't (do not).**
He/She/It **has** a book. He/She/It **doesn't (does not) have** a book.	**Q: Does** he/she/it **have** a book? **A: Yes,** he/she/it **does.** **No,** he/she/it **doesn't (does not).**

We use **have** and **has**

*   for things we own or possess.

    *I **have** three books.*   *She **has** a computer.*

*   to describe people, places, and things.

    *Libraries **have** many books.*   *The book **has** a green cover.*

*   for family and people we know.

    *I **have** a brother.*   *He **has** a friend in Canada.*

*   with expressions like: *have a cold/the flu*, *have a headache*, *have a problem*, and *have a good time*.

A. *Complete the sentences with the correct form of the verb* to be *or* to have.

1. Tony _____ twenty-two years old.
2. He _____ a job in a bookstore.
3. He _____ (negative) a car.
4. He _____ three brothers and one sister.
5. He also _____ a friend.
6. His name _____ Miguel.
7. They _____ a good time together.

B. *Work with a partner. Find out about your partner's age, friends, family, and things he or she has. Tell the class.*

PRONUNCIATION

-TEEN AND *-TY*

A. *Listen and repeat the numbers.*

1. 13 / 30   5. 17 / 70
2. 14 / 40   6. 18 / 80
3. 15 / 50   7. 19 / 90
4. 16 / 60

B. *Listen and circle the numbers you hear.*

1. 14 / 40   2. 15 / 50   3. 16 / 60   4. 17 / 70

CONVERSATION

A. *Listen to the conversation. Then listen again and repeat.*

Pablo: Do you have a book that's good for the beach?

Carol: Well, there are <u>all kinds of</u> books here. Look, here's my favorite comic book. It's great!

Pablo: No, thanks. <u>I'm not into</u> comic books.

Carol: Well, <u>you never know</u>. You might like this one.

Do you know these expressions? What do you think they mean?

all kinds of   I'm not into   you never know

B. *Work with a partner. Practice a part of the conversation. Replace the underlined words with the words below.*

Pablo: Do you have a book that's good for the beach?

Carol: Well, there are <u>all kinds of</u> books here. Look, here's my favorite comic book. It's great!

many different   a lot of

C. Your Turn. *Write a new conversation. Use some of the words below and your own ideas. Practice the conversation with a partner.*

all kinds of   I'm not into   you never know

 *Go to page 151 for the Internet Activity.*

<table>
<tr><td rowspan="3">DID YOU KNOW?</td><td>• The Da Vinci Code is the best-selling adult novel of all time for a one-year period. It sold 6 million copies.</td><td rowspan="3"></td></tr>
<tr><td>• Kazuko Hosoki, the equivalent of Oprah in Japan, wrote 81 books on fortune telling that sold a total of 34 million copies.</td></tr>
<tr><td>• The seventh, or last, book of the Harry Potter series sold 15 million copies in the first 24 hours it was on sale.</td></tr>
</table>

WHAT DO YOU KNOW ABOUT NEW YEAR'S GREETINGS?

謹賀

謹賀新

旧年中は格別のお引立てを賜り
心から御礼申しあげます
本年も変わらぬご愛顧のほどお願い申しあげます
二〇〇二年元旦

before you listen

Answer these questions.

1. What kinds of holiday greeting cards are there today?

2. Do you send holiday cards?

3. When do you send them?

VOCABULARY

MEANING

🎧 *Listen to the talk. Then write the correct words in the blanks.*

bundle	mailboxes	prepaid	separate
electronics	postcards	presents	temporary

1. I'm working at a _____ job that is only for one month.
2. People say there is a _____ of money, all tied up together, in that old house.
3. The British put their letters into red _____ that are along the streets.
4. That store sells computers, cell phones, and other _____.
5. Those plates and dishes are the most beautiful wedding _____ on the table.
6. I always _____ the light-colored clothes from the dark-colored clothes when I do laundry.
7. I'm buying _____ minutes for my phone so I have them when I go on vacation.
8. In Japan, some people send _____ for New Year's Day.

WORDS THAT GO TOGETHER

Write the correct words in the blanks.

lottery numbers	New Year's Day	postal service

1. Many people do not work on _____.
2. The _____ in our town puts our mail in a box near our front door.
3. I hope my ticket has the winning _____.

USE

Work with a partner to answer the questions. Use complete sentences.

1. What do the *mailboxes* in your country look like?
2. When do you receive *presents*?

(continued)

3. When do you send *postcards*?

4. What do you *separate*?

5. What *electronics* do you own?

6. What is *temporary*?

7. What does the *postal service* do in your country?

8. What do you like to do on *New Year's Day*?

COMPREHENSION: LONG TALK

UNDERSTANDING THE LISTENING

Listen to the talk. Then circle the letter of the correct answer.

1. What are *nengajo* cards?

    a. New Year's cards for Japanese friends and family

    b. New Year's photos for Japanese family members

    c. New Year's presents for co-workers

2. Which is NOT a way postal workers separate New Year's cards from regular mail?

    a. They look for the mail with a picture of electronics on it.

    b. They look for the mail with the word "nenga" under the stamp.

    c. They look for the prepaid postcards.

3. How do the Japanese open their cards?

    a. They open as many as possible before New Year's Day.

    b. They open one every day between December 15 and December 25.

    c. They open them all at once on New Year's Day.

REMEMBERING DETAILS

Listen to the talk again. Then answer these questions.

1. Who do the Japanese send *nengajo* cards to?

2. What kind of photos do they put on the *nengajo* cards?

3. When do people receive their *nengajo* cards?

4. Where do people put their *nengajo* cards?

5. What do people with the winning *lottery numbers* get?

6. How do people feel when they open their *nengajo* cards?

🎧 TAKING NOTES: Cards

Listen and write notes about the description. Which card does it describe?

eCard

paper card

COMPREHENSION: SHORT CONVERSATIONS

🎧 *Listen to the conversations. Then circle the letter of the correct answer.*

CONVERSATION 1

1. Who is the woman talking to?

  a. a friend   **b.** a salesman in a shop   **c.** an art teacher

CONVERSATION 2

2. Why is the man unhappy?

  a. His mail is always late.   **b.** He's not getting his mail.   **c.** He's getting other people's mail.

CONVERSATION 3

3. What is the woman shopping for?

  a. a cell phone   **b.** a DVD player   **c.** an MP3 player

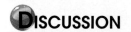

DISCUSSION

Discuss the answers to these questions with your classmates.

1. At what times do people give cards and gifts in your country? What are some traditional gifts that they give on certain occasions?

2. What are some traditions in your country for giving good wishes to others? When and how do you give these wishes? Why are they important?

3. What does a new year mean to you? How do you like to celebrate the beginning of a new year?

CRITICAL THINKING

Work with a partner. Ask each other the following questions. Discuss your answers.

1. Why do people like to send and receive cards and gifts? Which is better, to give or to receive? Why?

2. In today's electronic age, not as many people send cards or letters as in the past. What are the good and bad sides of electronic communication? What are the good and bad sides of letters and other postal greetings?

LANGUAGE FOCUS

PRESENT PROGRESSIVE

Statements	Questions and Answers
I'm writing cards. I'm not writing cards.	Q: Am I writing cards? A: Yes, I am. No, I'm not.
He's/She's writing cards. He/She isn't writing cards.	Q: Is he/she writing cards? A: Yes, he/she is. No, he/she isn't.
We're/You're/They're writing cards. We/You/They aren't writing cards.	Q: Are we/you/they writing cards? A: Yes, we/you/they are. No, we/you/they aren't.

- We use the **present progressive** to talk about what is happening now or around the time of speaking.
- We use these time words with the present progressive: *now, at the moment, today, this week, these days.*
- We do not use some verbs in the present progressive because they do not describe an action. Here are some verbs we do not use in the present progressive: *see, prefer, know, understand, need.*

Spelling rules: study→*studying*   write→*writing*   shop→*shopping*

A. *Complete the sentences with the correct form of the verbs.*

1. I (like) _____ these cards.

2. What are you (do) _____ this week?

3. I (need) _____ a phone.

4. They (have) _____ special mailboxes for New Year's cards.

5. Who are you (wait) _____ for?

6. It's (rain) _____ outside at the moment.

7. She's (write) _____ cards right now.

8. Is your sister (come) _____ too?

B. *Work with a partner. Describe what a student is wearing and doing in your class. Do not say the name of the student. Your partner guesses who it is.*

EXAMPLE:

A: This student is wearing a white shirt.

B: Is it Andy?

A: No, it isn't. This student is sitting next to the window.

PRONUNCIATION

TH AND *T*

🎧 **A.** *Listen and notice the sounds* th *and* t*. Then listen again and repeat.*

1. thanks / tanks
2. tenth / tent

3. three / tree
4. fourth / fort

B. *Listen and circle the word you hear.*

1. math / mat
2. thin / tin
3. thanks / tanks

4. sheet / sheath
5. fourth / fort

CONVERSATION

 A. *Listen to the conversation. Then listen again and repeat.*

Emma: <u>My goodness</u>, what's that?

Chris: It's a present for my brother. I have another one, too. His birthday is tomorrow.

Emma: <u>Really?</u> You're giving him both presents <u>at once</u>?

Chris: That's right. I'm putting them together in one large bundle.

Do you know these expressions? What do you think they mean?

My goodness   Really?   at once

B. *Work with a partner. Practice a part of the conversation. Replace the underlined words with the words below.*

Emma: <u>My goodness</u>, what's that?

Chris: It's a present for my brother. I have another one, too. His birthday is tomorrow.

Wow   Oh, my

C. Your Turn. *Write a new conversation. Use some of the words below and your own ideas. Practice the conversation with a partner.*

My goodness   Really?   at once

 Go to page 151 for the Internet Activity.

WHAT DO YOU KNOW ABOUT FAMOUS PALACES?

you listen

Answer these questions.

1. What are some palaces from around the world?

2. Who usually lives in palaces?

3. Where does the leader of your country live?

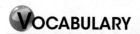VOCABULARY

MEANING

🎧 *Listen to the talk. Then write the correct words in the blanks.*

collection	elevators	lawns	rug
drapes	flags	oval	staircases

1. An egg has an ___OVal___ shape.
2. The girl puts her ___Collection___ of dolls in the closet.
3. The blue ___rug___ looks beautiful in the room.
4. Rain makes the grass on the ___lawns___ a deep green.
5. The workers use two ___Staircases___ to ride to the top floor.
6. The ___elevators___ on the houses lead up to the front doors.
7. The ___drapes___ over the windows keep the sun out of the room.
8. We have two ___flags___ on poles in front of our building.

WORDS THAT GO TOGETHER

Write the correct words in the blanks.

free of charge	gives a speech	take a tour

1. The museum is ___free of charge___ today, so no one pays any money.
2. I want to ___take a tour___ of Moscow and see all the beautiful buildings.
3. The president of the school ___gives a speech___ to welcome the students.

USE

Work with a partner to answer the questions. Use complete sentences.

1. Where do you want to *take a tour*? I want to take a tour on this bilding
2. Where is there a *rug* in your house? the rug is on my room
3. What color are the *drapes* in your living room? the color for drapsare white
4. What has an *oval* shape? the egg has oval shape.
5. What *collection* do you have?
   I like to collection cars.

16 UNIT 3

6. What do you like about *flags*? I like my cuntriy flags
7. What do *elevators* help us do? The elevators help us to clime to the top.
8. Why do some people like to use *staircases*? They use staircases must People to exts.

COMPREHENSION: LONG TALK

UNDERSTANDING THE LISTENING

Listen to the talk. Then circle the letter of the correct answer.

1. What do visitors see at the White House?

   (a.) many rooms and gardens
   b. a museum with famous paintings
   c. drapes and rugs from Queen Victoria

2. What does the president do in the Oval Office?

   a. watches television
   (b.) works
   c. talks with friends and family

3. What is the desk in the Oval Office made from?

   (a.) wood from a ship
   b. wood from a famous tree
   c. wood from Queen Victoria's desk

REMEMBERING DETAILS

Listen to the talk again. Then write the correct words in the blanks.

1. Visitors can __take atour__ of the White House free of charge.
2. Sometimes the president __give a speech__ from the lawn of the White House.
3. The president works from the __oval office__.
4. The president chooses __Painting s__ from the White House collection.
5. No president changes the __flags__ in the Oval Office.
6. The desk in the Oval Office is a gift from the queen of __England__.

TAKING NOTES: Palaces

Listen and write notes about the description. Which palace does it describe?

Schönbrunn Palace, Austria

Palace of Versailles, France

COMPREHENSION: SHORT CONVERSATIONS

Listen to the conversations. Then circle the letter of the correct answer.

CONVERSATION 1

1. What does the man do at the palace?

   a. He is a visitor.   **b.** He lives there.   **c.** He works there.

CONVERSATION 2

2. Who is the woman talking to?

   a. her friend   **b.** a salesman   **c.** a bank worker

CONVERSATION 3

3. What does the woman want to do?

   a. hear the queen's speech   **b.** see the inside of the palace   **c.** see the gardens

DISCUSSION

Discuss the answers to these questions with your classmates.

1. Do you like to take tours of famous buildings? Why or why not?
2. Where do you like to visit the most? Why?
3. If the Oval Office is yours, what does it look like? What colors are the drapes, walls, and rugs? What kind of furniture is in the room? What kinds of paintings are there?

CRITICAL THINKING

Work with a partner. Ask each other the following questions. Discuss your answers.

1. How is life in a palace different from life in most people's homes? Which do you like best?

2. What do you think life is like for a world leader like the president of the United States? What are the good parts? What are the hard parts?

LANGUAGE FOCUS

SIMPLE PRESENT

Statements	Questions and Answers
I/We/You/They **live** in a palace.	**Q:** **Do** I/we/you/they **live** in a palace? **A:** **Yes,** I/we/you/they **do live** in a palace. **No,** I/we/you/they **don't (do not) live** in a palace.
He/She/It **lives** in a palace.	**Q:** **Does** he/she/it **live** in a palace? **A:** **Yes,** he/she/it **does live** in a palace. **No,** he/she/it **doesn't (does not) live** in a palace.

We use the **simple present** to talk about what people do all the time or again and again.

The president lives in the White House.

A. *Write questions about the White House with these words. Then answer the questions with complete sentences.*

1. the president / live in the White House?

   Does the president live in the White House? Yes, he does live in the White House.

2. visitors / pay to take a tour of the White House?

   _____

3. How many / rooms / White House have?

   _____

(continued)

4. Where / the president / give a speech?

_____

5. Where / the president / work?

_____

6. Who / the president / meet in the Oval Office?

_____

B. *Work with a partner. Tell your partner four things you* do *and four things you* don't do *on the weekend. Use the words below or your own words.*

do homework   get up early   see friends   study English   walk the dog

PRONUNCIATION

THIRD PERSON -*S*

A. *Listen and notice the final -s sound. Then listen again and repeat.*

/s/	/z/	/ɪz/
1. works	**3.** lives	**5.** chooses
2. walks	**4.** gives	**6.** changes

B. *Listen and check the final -s sound you hear.*

	/s/	/z/	/ɪz/
1. The president **lives** there.		✓	
2. He **likes** his desk.		✓	
3. He **reads** letters there.		✓	
4. He **sits** at his desk.	✓		
5. He **changes** the furniture.			✓
6. He **watches** the people from his window.			✓

# CONVERSATION

 A. *Listen to the conversation. Then listen again and repeat.*

> **Sam:** Is that a picture of you at Buckingham Palace?
> **Brad:** <u>Believe it or not</u>, it is. <u>Like you</u>, I love London.
> **Sam:** Do you know the queen has many other homes?
> **Brad:** <u>Well,</u> yes. And many of them are palaces!

Do you know these expressions? What do you think they mean?

Believe it or not   Like you   Well,

B. *Work with a partner. Practice a part of the conversation. Replace the underlined words with the words below.*

> **Sam:** Is that a picture of you at Buckingham Palace?
> **Brad:** <u>Believe it or not</u>, it is. Like you, I love London.

Certainly   ⟨ Of course ⟩

C. **Your Turn.** *Write a new conversation. Use some of the words below and your own ideas. Practice the conversation with a partner.*

Believe it or not   Like you   Well,

 Go to page 151 for the Internet Activity.

DID YOU KNOW?	• The house of the president of the United States was originally gray. Its name changed to the White House after workers painted it white to cover the fire damage caused by the British in the War of 1812. • The Forbidden City, a palace in China, has 9,999 rooms. Nine is a lucky number for the Chinese. • The Palace of Versailles in France is the largest palace in Europe and took fifty years to build.	

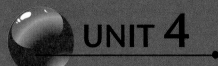

WHAT ANIMALS ARE USEFUL TO HUMANS?

before you listen

Answer these questions.

1. What is an animal that is useful to humans in many ways?

2. In what ways is a cow useful?

3. How are pets useful to humans?

VOCABULARY

MEANING

Listen to the talk. Then write the correct words in the blanks.

ashes	fuel	sacred	tractors
fertilizer	produce	survive	utensils

1. Farmers put _____ in the ground to make the plants grow better.

2. People use _____ so that they don't have to eat with their hands.

3. Our trees always _____ lots of fruit in the summer.

4. Every animal needs to eat to _____.

5. We usually use a lot of _____ to give us heat in the winter.

6. After we burn our wood, there are always _____ in the fireplace.

7. _____ help farmers to work in the fields.

8. Cows are very special to many people in India. They are _____.

WORDS THAT GO TOGETHER

Write the correct words in the blanks.

depend on	family member	plow the field

1. Many humans all over the world _____ animals for food.

2. When farmers _____, they cut into the soil so they can plant their seeds.

3. My grandfather is my favorite _____.

USE

Work with a partner to answer the questions. Use complete sentences.

1. At what time of year does a farmer usually *plow the field*?

2. How do people *survive* in the desert?

3. Why does farmland need *fertilizer*?

4. What is *sacred* to you?

5. Why is it always important to put water on *ashes* from a fire?

(continued)

6. What animals *produce* many babies every year?

7. What *utensils* do you use when you eat?

8. How many *family members* live in your home?

COMPREHENSION: LONG TALK

UNDERSTANDING THE LISTENING

🎧 *Listen to the talk. Then circle the letter of the correct answer.*

1. Why are cows sacred to Hindus?

   a. They give Hindus many things.
   b. They help make people rich in the countryside.
   c. They give meat for people to eat.

2. How do farmers use the male cows?

   a. for milk
   b. for help in the fields
   c. for cheese and butter

3. What are some uses for cow dung?

   a. fuel and fertilizer
   b. food and bricks
   c. utensils and cooking

REMEMBERING DETAILS

🎧 *Listen to the talk again. Circle T if the sentence is true. Circle F if the sentence is false.*

1. Hindus like to eat meat.	T	F
2. Cows are not important to Hindus.	T	F
3. People in the countryside in India usually have two or three cows.	T	F
4. Many farmers in India use oxen to plow the fields.	T	F
5. Cow dung burns very fast.	T	F
6. In India, some people use cow dung to build their houses.	T	F

TAKING NOTES: Animals

🎧 *Listen and write notes about the description. Which animal does it describe?*

camel

llama

COMPREHENSION: SHORT CONVERSATIONS

🎧 *Listen to the conversations. Then circle the letter of the correct answer.*

CONVERSATION 1

1. Where is the man going?

   a. to the ocean   **b.** to the city   **c.** to the countryside

CONVERSATION 2

2. Why is the woman unhappy?

   a. There's no fuel for their fire.   **b.** It's getting dark outside.   **c.** The man is late to cut the wood.

CONVERSATION 3

3. What does the woman use her horses for?

   a. pleasure   **b.** to plow the fields   **c.** to pull the tractor

DISCUSSION

Discuss the answers to these questions with your classmates.

1. What is your favorite animal? Why?
2. How are animals useful to humans other than as food?
3. What animals are dangerous to humans? Why is it important to protect even the dangerous animals on Earth?

 CRITICAL THINKING

Work with a partner. Ask each other the following questions. Discuss your answers.

1. Do you eat meat or are you a vegetarian (a person that doesn't eat meat)? What are some reasons why people are vegetarians? Do you think it's wrong to eat meat? Why or why not?

2. Many cultures in history and today believe that certain animals are sacred, such as the cat in ancient Egypt, the bear and wolf for Native Americans in the United States, and the tiger in China. What do humans see in animals that is so special? What animals do people in your culture think are special? What animal do you think is special? Why?

 LANGUAGE FOCUS

SIMPLE PRESENT WITH ADVERBS OF FREQUENCY

0% _____ 100%

| never | seldom/rarely | sometimes | often | usually | always |

- *Never, seldom/rarely, sometimes, often, usually,* and *always* are **adverbs of frequency**. They tell us how often something happens.
- In statements in the simple present, adverbs of frequency come before the main verb, but they come after the verb *to be.*

I	**always** eat meat.
He/She/It	**always** eats meat.
We/You/They	**always** eat meat.

I	am **usually** hungry.
He/She/It	is **usually** hungry.
We/You/They	are **usually** hungry.

- In questions, adverbs of frequency come after the subject.

   Do you always eat meat?
   When do they usually eat dinner?

A. *Rewrite the sentences with the adverb of frequency.*

1. A family has one cow. (usually)

   A family usually has one cow.

2. A farmer uses oxen to plow the field. (often)

   _____

3. They use dung to make houses. (sometimes)

   _____

4. The cow is like a member of the family. (usually)

   _____

5. The cow is important for a Hindu family. (always)

   _____

6. They kill their cows. (never)

   _____

B. *Work with a partner. What do you do on weekday evenings? Use* always, usually, often, sometimes, *and* never *with these phrases.*

stay at home	go to bed late	send text messages	play video games
watch television	do homework	eat out	meet friends

EXAMPLE:

A: I usually stay at home on weekday evenings.

B: I always go to bed late on weekday evenings.

PRONUNCIATION

REDUCED FORM OF *DO* AND *DOES*

A. *Listen to the questions. Notice the reduced form of* do *and* does. *Circle the words you hear. Then listen again and repeat.*

EXAMPLE:

When do you get up?

What time does he get up?

1. What (do you / do they) use to clean utensils?
2. When (do we / does he) usually go to the movies?
3. What time (does he / does she) come home from school?

(continued)

4. When (do you / do they) meet your friends?

5. What (does he / do we) have for breakfast?

6. What fuel (do you / do we) use to cook food?

B. *Work with a partner. Write and ask four questions with an adverb of frequency for your partner to answer. Try to use the reduced form of* do *and* does.

CONVERSATION

A. *Listen to the conversation. Then listen again and repeat.*

Anjali: My new puppy is an Australian cattle dog.

Dan: <u>No way!</u> Those dogs are <u>just like</u> horses. They keep the cows all together in a group.

Anjali: Yes, they're very smart dogs. <u>What else</u> do you know about them?

Dan: Well, they're very strong. And they travel a long way over hot, dry areas of Australia.

Do you know these expressions? What do you think they mean?

No way!   just like   What else

B. *Work with a partner. Practice a part of the conversation. Replace the underlined words with the words below.*

Anjali: My new puppy is an Australian cattle dog.

Dan: <u>No way!</u> Those dogs are just like horses. They keep the cows all together in a group.

You're kidding!   I don't believe it!

C. Your Turn. *Write a new conversation. Use some of the words below and your own ideas. Practice the conversation with a partner.*

No way!   just like   What else

Go to page 152 for the Internet Activity.

| **DID YOU KNOW?** | • All cats and most dogs can't taste sugar.
• In the past, people tried to use horses, pigeons, camels, dogs, reindeer, and cats to deliver mail. The cat service didn't work.
• People use horse hair to make paintbrushes and violin bows. | |

WHAT DO YOU KNOW ABOUT GIFT GIVING?

before you listen

Answer these questions.

1. What kinds of gifts do you like to receive?
2. Who do you give gifts to most often?
3. Where is your favorite place to buy gifts?

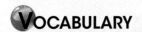

MEANING

Listen to the talk. Then write the correct words in the blanks.

appropriate	host	occasions	suitable
beliefs	modesty	respect	symbolizes

1. My parents teach us to treat our grandparents well and to show them _____.

2. We like to go out to dinner for special _____.

3. In many cultures, the color black _____ death.

4. He is an excellent _____. We always have fun at his parties.

5. Red is a _____ color for your dress because this is a happy and bright time of the year.

6. Different cultures have different _____ about what happens to people after they die.

7. People who show _____ do not try to bring attention to themselves.

8. Sid always knows the _____ gift to give at a wedding.

WORDS THAT GO TOGETHER

Write the correct words in the blanks.

gift giving	give up	make a suggestion

1. She asks her mother to _____ about what gift to take to the party.

2. I don't want you to _____ your studies because it's important to keep trying.

3. The _____ is over, so now all the guests have something to take home with them.

USE

Work with a partner to answer the questions. Use complete sentences.

1. When do you feel like you want to *give up*?

2. What clothes are *suitable* for cold weather?

3. When do you enjoy *gift giving*?

4. What are your favorite family *occasions*?

5. What is something that a *host* usually does?

6. What is an *appropriate* gift for a small child?

7. What are some of your strong *beliefs*?

8. How do you show *respect* for a teacher?

COMPREHENSION: LONG TALK

UNDERSTANDING THE LISTENING

Listen to the talk. Then circle the letter of the correct answer.

1. Before you give a gift to your host, what is it important to know?

   a. the language he or she speaks
   b. the customs of his or her country
   c. what he or she is serving for dinner

2. Why is it important to choose the color of wrapping paper carefully?

   a. Colors have different meanings in different cultures.
   b. Bright colors always show friendship.
   c. Some people don't like colors.

3. Why may a Japanese person refuse a gift that you give them?

   a. They think gift giving is not appropriate.
   b. They want to be polite.
   c. Gifts remind them of sad occasions.

REMEMBERING DETAILS

Listen to the talk again. Then answer these questions.

1. Why is gift giving important to the Japanese?

2. Why isn't it a good idea to give a clock as a gift in China?

3. What does a pen symbolize in China?

4. What is a good gift to give in Japanese culture?

5. Why is the presentation of a gift important in Japanese culture?

6. What does the color red symbolize to the Japanese?

TAKING NOTES: Gifts

🎧 *Listen and write notes about the description. Which gift does it describe?*

Valentine's Day gift

birthday gift

COMPREHENSION: SHORT CONVERSATIONS

🎧 *Listen to the conversations. Then circle the letter of the correct answer.*

CONVERSATION 1

1. Why doesn't the woman know what to buy for her brother?

    a. He doesn't like gifts.

    b. He already has everything he needs.

    c. He wants too many things.

CONVERSATION 2

2. What is an appropriate gift for the woman to buy?

    a. a silver teapot

    b. towels

    c. a book about birds

CONVERSATION 3

3. Why is the man dressed so nicely?

    a. He has a job interview.

    b. He's going to a funeral.

    c. He's going to a wedding.

DISCUSSION

Discuss the answers to these questions with your classmates.

1. What are the gift-giving customs of your country? How do you present gifts to others? How do you wrap them? Are there gifts that are not appropriate, such as the clock in China? How do you receive gifts?

2. On what occasions do you usually give gifts to others? Do you like to give gifts? Why or why not? What is fun about gift giving? What is difficult?

3. What do you think are appropriate gifts for the following occasions: birth of a baby, wedding, Valentine's Day, dinner with a boss, a child's birthday? In your discussion, include other special days in your culture.

CRITICAL THINKING

Work with a partner. Ask each other the following questions. Discuss your answers.

1. What are some reasons why people give gifts to others? What shows thoughtfulness in a gift? What shows lack of thought? Why is it important to give an appropriate gift for each occasion?

2. Why is it important to know the customs of countries where you travel? What happens when you know the customs? What happens when you don't? What are some ways in which we can learn about other cultures before we travel?

LANGUAGE FOCUS

COMPARATIVE ADJECTIVES

We use **comparative adjectives** to compare two people or things. We use a comparative adjective + *than*.

Adjective Descriptions	Adjectives	Comparative Adjectives
short adjectives (1 syllable)	bright nice	brighter than nicer than
adjectives ending in -*y*	happy easy	happier than easier than
longer adjectives (2 or more syllables)	suitable polite	more suitable than more polite than
irregular adjectives	good bad	better than worse than

A. John and his friend Tom are guests for dinner at their boss's house. John is taking an expensive box of chocolates wrapped in beautiful light, bright colored paper with ribbons. Tom is taking a gift given to him which he hasn't opened. It is probably a vase or a dish. The wrapping paper is dark and old looking. Write the answers to the questions with complete sentences. Use comparative adjectives.

1. Whose gift is more suitable?

   John's gift is more suitable than Tom's.

2. Whose wrapping paper is better?

   _____

3. Whose box is brighter?

   _____

4. Whose gift is worse?

   _____

5. Which gift is nicer?

   _____

6. Which person is more thoughtful?

   _____

B. Work with a partner. Compare yourself with your partner using the words below and your own words.

darker than   shorter than   funnier than   more colorful than

PRONUNCIATION

-ER

We find this sound /ɚ/ mostly in words spelled with the letters *er*, *ar*, and *or*.

A. *Listen and notice the sound /ɚ/.*

1. That color is brighter.
2. This paper is lighter.
3. This sugar is sweeter.
4. This water is better.

B. *Listen and underline the sound /ɝ/ in the sentences.*

1. My father is older.
2. This flavor is stronger.
3. The weather is warmer.
4. This grammar is harder.

CONVERSATION

 A. *Listen to the conversation. Then listen again and repeat.*

Sara: Do you have a gift for Peter? It's his birthday tomorrow.

Max: Well, <u>that's news to me</u>. I don't have a gift, and now I don't know what to do.

Sara: <u>No problem!</u> I'm very good at shopping. Do you want me to help you?

Max: <u>Absolutely!</u> You know, it's funny. I love to shop until I have to buy for someone else!

Do you know these expressions? What do you think they mean?

> that's news to me   No problem!   Absolutely!

B. *Work with a partner. Practice a part of the conversation. Replace the underlined words with the words below.*

Sara: Do you have a gift for Peter? It's his birthday tomorrow.

Max: Well, <u>that's news to me</u>. I don't have a gift, and now I don't know what to do.

> this is the first I hear about it   that's a surprise

C. Your Turn. *Write a new conversation. Use some of the words below and your own ideas. Practice the conversation with a partner.*

> that's news to me   No problem!   Absolutely!

 *Go to page 152 for the Internet Activity.*

DID YOU KNOW?

- In the United States, people open gifts in front of the person who gives the gift; however, in most Asian countries people open gifts when the giver is not present.
- If a German invites you to his or her home, bring a gift such as chocolates or flowers. Yellow roses or tea roses are good, but red roses symbolize romantic intentions, and carnations symbolize mourning.
- In South Korea, cash is a popular gift for weddings. People put gifts of money in white envelopes.

UNIT 6

WHAT ARE SOME TYPICAL FOODS FROM AROUND THE WORLD?

before you listen

Answer these questions.

1. What is the food you think of when people say these countries:

   Italy, Mexico, Japan, the United States, India

2. What is a popular food in your country?

3. What is your favorite food from another country?

VOCABULARY

MEANING

Listen to the talk. Then write the correct words in the blanks.

cabbage	radishes	region	spicy
cucumbers	recipe	sour	tastes

1. I live in a _____ of my country that has many mountains and rivers.

2. I love the hot taste and strong smell of _____ food.

3. _____ are long fruits that are dark green on the outside and white on the inside.

4. Sweet and salty are only two of the many different _____ of food.

5. My _____ for tomato soup tells you everything you need to make it.

6. This year, I'm growing some _____—the small round ones with bright red skin.

7. This green apple is as _____ as a lemon!

8. A _____ is round and has big green, white, or red leaves.

WORDS THAT GO TOGETHER

Write the correct words in the blanks.

in season	modern times	to get together

1. My friends and I love _____ and play soccer in the park.

2. We eat lots of peaches during the summer, which is when they are

   _____.

3. We are living in _____—life is very different than before.

USE

Work with a partner to answer the questions. Use complete sentences.

1. What *region* of your country has the most water?

2. Who do you like *to get together* with?

3. Where can people find many *recipes*?

(continued)

4. What fruits are *in season* during the summer in your country?

5. What are some different *tastes* of chocolate?

6. What is an example of a *spicy* food?

7. In what part of the plant do *radishes* grow?

8. What fruit or vegetable tastes *sour*?

COMPREHENSION: LONG TALK

UNDERSTANDING THE LISTENING

🎧 *Listen to the talk. Then circle the letter of the correct answer.*

1. In what way is kimchi the same for all Koreans?

    a. It's hot and spicy.   **b.** It has vegetables and spices.   **c.** It's sweet and salty.

2. What tradition often decides what someone uses to make kimchi?

    a. the time of year   **b.** the number of family members and friends   **c.** the kind of holiday

3. What tradition is popular with friends and families in October or November?

    a. They all go to the farm and buy food to make kimchi.   **b.** They all make kimchi together in a home.   **c.** They sell jars of kimchi to each other.

REMEMBERING DETAILS

🎧 *Listen to the talk again. Circle* **T** *if the sentence is true. Circle* **F** *if the sentence is false.*

1. Koreans eat kimchi every day.	T	F
2. Everyone in a region eats the same kind of kimchi.	T	F
3. Fish kimchi is the most popular kind of kimchi.	T	F
4. Radishes are in season in the summer.	T	F
5. It takes two to three weeks to prepare 100 to 200 cabbages.	T	F
6. Families don't practice kimchi traditions anymore.	T	F

TAKING NOTES: Foods

🎧 *Listen and write notes about the description. Which food does it describe?*

pasta

sushi

COMPREHENSION: SHORT CONVERSATIONS

🎧 *Listen to the conversations. Then circle the letter of the correct answer.*

CONVERSATION 1

1. Why is the man unhappy?

   a. He has guests coming.
   b. He doesn't want to serve cucumbers.
   c. There aren't any good cucumbers.

CONVERSATION 2

2. Who is the woman talking to?

   a. her friend
   b. her waiter
   c. the cook

CONVERSATION 3

3. Where is the woman?

   a. at a market
   b. at a farm
   c. at a restaurant

DISCUSSION

Discuss the answers to these questions with your classmates.

1. What foods do you like to eat? Do you like to try different kinds of foods? Why or why not? Do you want to try kimchi? Why or why not?

2. How many different regions are there in your country? How are they different in the way they look and the people who live there?

3. How are these regions different in the kind of food people eat and the way they prepare it?

CRITICAL THINKING

Work with a partner. Ask each other the following questions. Discuss your answers.

1. What foods do older people in your country like? What foods do younger people like? Do you think the tastes of young people are changing? Why or why not? What influences young people's tastes today? What other tastes do young people have that are different from their elders?

2. Why are traditions important? Which traditions in your country do you enjoy? Which traditions do you want to keep? Which traditions do you want to change? Why?

LANGUAGE FOCUS

COUNT AND NON-COUNT NOUNS

COUNT NOUNS		NON-COUNT NOUNS	
Singular	**Plural**	**Singular**	**Plural**
a cucumber	cucumbers	rice	———
a radish	radishes	salt	———
one cabbage	three cabbages	meat	———

In English, there are **count nouns** and **non-count nouns**. Count nouns are singular and plural. Non-count nouns are always singular. We use *some* and *any* with count and non-count nouns.

- We use *some* in positive statements.

  I want some pasta.

- We use *any* in negative statements.

  I don't want any pasta.

- We use *any* in questions.

  Do you want any pasta?

A. *Complete the sentences with* some *or* any.

1. I have _____ radishes and onions.

2. We don't have _____ garlic.

3. Do we have _____ ginger?

4. Is there _____ salt on this?

5. I want _____ pizza.

6. She can have _____ chicken.

B. *Work with a partner. Think of five things you buy in a supermarket and five things you don't buy. Use complete sentences. Use* some *and* any *when necessary.*

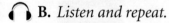
PRONUNCIATION

REDUCED FORM OF *AND*

 A. *Listen and notice the sound of* and. *Then listen again and repeat.*

We write	We say
1. salt and pepper	2. salt 'n' pepper
3. sweet and sour	4. sweet 'n' sour
5. hot and spicy	6. hot 'n' spicy

B. *Listen and repeat.*

1. I love fruits and vegetables.
2. They put garlic and ginger in kimchi.
3. In Mexico they like rice and beans.
4. The English have fish and chips.
5. The Americans like hamburgers and fries.
6. The French are famous for their wine and cheese.

CONVERSATION

A. *Listen to the conversation. Then listen again and repeat.*

Fran: <u>How about that?</u> You're finally eating sushi! What's it like?

Eric: No, this is cooked fish, not sushi. So, <u>of course</u>, it's delicious!

(continued)

Fran: <u>That's too bad.</u> You never want to try anything new.

Eric: That's true. I want to change but I just can't do it!

Do you know these expressions? What do you think they mean?

How about that?   of course   That's too bad.

B. *Work with a partner. Practice a part of the conversation. Replace the underlined words with the words below.*

Fran: <u>How about that?</u> You're finally eating sushi! What's it like?

Eric: No, this is cooked fish, not sushi. So, of course, it's delicious!

Look at you!   I don't believe it!

C. **Your Turn.** *Write a new conversation. Use some of the words below and your own ideas. Practice the conversation with a partner.*

How about that?   of course   That's too bad.

 Go to page 153 for the Internet Activity.

<table>
<tr>
<td>DID
YOU
KNOW?</td>
<td>

- Three billion people in the world eat rice as the main food in their diet. The world population is almost seven billion.
- In the Middle East, fast food is a falafel stand and in Asia it's a noodle shop.
- The Greeks are the world's biggest consumers per person of olive oil.

</td>
<td></td>
</tr>
</table>

WHAT DO YOU KNOW ABOUT NORTHERN EUROPE?

you listen

Answer these questions.

1. What are some countries in Northern Europe?

2. What do you think of when you think of countries like Norway and Sweden?

3. When do you think is a good time to go to Northern Europe, summer or winter? Why?

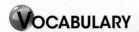

VOCABULARY

MEANING

🎧 *Listen to the talk. Then write the correct words in the blanks.*

adventure	design	melt	spectacular
chapel	grand	sculptures	unique

1. That building is so beautiful that it is truly _____.

2. This exciting and dangerous mountain climb is quite an _____.

3. Before I make my dress, I'm going to draw its _____.

4. This hotel is _____. There isn't another one like it.

5. It's such a warm day that my ice cream is going to _____ fast.

6. My brother cuts pieces out of wood and makes beautiful animal

   _____.

7. That large and beautiful opera house is very _____.

8. There is a little _____ by the lake where my friends are going to get

   married.

WORDS THAT GO TOGETHER

Write the correct words in the blanks.

below freezing	have reservations	work of art

1. We _____ for two rooms at a hotel tonight.

2. This painting is the most special _____ that I own.

3. The ice on the lake is thick because the temperatures are

   _____.

USE

Work with a partner to answer the questions. Use complete sentences.

1. Where in your country are there *spectacular* places to see?

2. Who do you know that likes *adventure*?

3. What place has temperatures that are *below freezing* much of the time?

4. Why is it good to *have reservations* before you take a trip?

5. What *work of art* do you like?

6. Where do we often see *sculptures*?

7. What causes ice to *melt*?

8. What is your favorite *design* for a hotel?

COMPREHENSION: LONG TALK

UNDERSTANDING THE LISTENING

Listen to the talk. Then circle the letter of the correct answer.

1. Why are the man and his wife going to Sweden?

   a. They love adventure.
   b. They don't know anywhere else to go.
   c. They love cold weather.

2. What changes at the Ice Hotel every year?

   a. where the owners build it
   b. what it looks like
   c. what the builders use to make it

3. What do guests find when they go to the Ice Hotel?

   a. beautiful paintings
   b. warm beds
   c. ice tables and chairs

REMEMBERING DETAILS

Listen to the talk again. Then write the correct words in the blanks.

1. The Ice Hotel is made of _____.

2. Workers make a new Ice Hotel _____ a year.

3. The workers get the ice to build the hotel from a _____.

4. In the _____ there is an ice chandelier.

5. The Ice Hotel has an ice chapel for _____.

6. Visitors at the Ice Hotel wear special _____ to stay warm.

TAKING NOTES: Transportation

🎧 *Listen and write notes about the description. Which form of transportation does it describe?*

dog sledding

horse sledding

COMPREHENSION: SHORT CONVERSATIONS

🎧 *Listen to the conversations. Then circle the letter of the correct answer.*

CONVERSATION 1

1. What is the best place for the man to go on his ski trip?

   a. Pine Mountain   **b.** Black Mountain   **c.** White Mountain

CONVERSATION 2

2. What is the man going to do?

   a. look for his gloves   **b.** take a taxi   **c.** leave without his gloves

CONVERSATION 3

3. What is the woman going to do?

   a. find another hotel   **b.** talk to the manager   **c.** write to the author

DISCUSSION

Discuss the answers to these questions with your classmates.

1. What are some unusual places to visit in the world? Which places do you want to see? Why?

2. Do you like adventure? Why or why not? What is the most exciting thing you ever saw or did? Where do you dream of going? Why?

3. Why do you think so many people go to see the Ice Hotel? What parts of staying at the hotel sound interesting and fun? What parts don't? Do you want to go and stay at the Ice Hotel? Why or why not?

CRITICAL THINKING

Work with a partner. Ask each other the following questions. Discuss your answers.

1. Many people today like to do adventure travel. What is adventure travel? What are some examples of adventure travel trips? Why do you think so many people want to do these trips today? What kind of people like adventure travel?

2. Imagine you are going to build a unique hotel. Where is it and what does it look like? Why do people want to go there?

LANGUAGE FOCUS

BE GOING TO

Statements	Questions and Answers
I'm (am) going to ski. I'm (am) not going to ski.	Q: Am I going to ski? A: Yes, I am. No, I'm (am) not.
He/She/It's (is) going to ski. He/She/It isn't (is not) going to ski.	Q: Is he/she/it going to ski? A: Yes, he/she/it is. No, he/she/it isn't (is not).
You/We/They're (are) going to ski. You/We/They aren't (are not) going to ski.	Q: Are you/we/they going to ski? A: Yes, you/we/they are. No, you/we/they aren't (are not).

We use **be going to**

- for plans for the future.

    They're going to stay at the Ice Hotel in December.

- for predictions about the future.

    It's going to be cold tomorrow.

A. *What is going to happen? Look at the situation and write a sentence with* be going to.

1. He's putting on his skis.

    He's going to ski.

2. She has her wedding dress on, and he has a dark suit on. They're going to the chapel.

_____

(continued)

3. He looks at the bill and is giving his credit card to the hotel clerk.

_____

4. She's thirsty. She asks for a glass of water.

_____

5. He turns off his computer and the lights. He wants to go home.

_____

6. They're in the airport at the gate ready to go. The plane is boarding in a few minutes.

_____

B. _Work with a partner. Say five things you are going to do or not going to do this winter or next winter._

PRONUNCIATION

REDUCED FORM OF *BE GOING TO*

A. _Listen and notice the sound of_ be going to. _Then listen again and repeat._

1. He's going to ski tomorrow.
2. We're going to have fun.
3. You're going to freeze there.
4. They're going to come back this week.

B. _Listen to the sentences and write the missing words you hear._

1. The ice _____.
2. It's _____ tonight.
3. She's _____ in winter.
4. They're _____ at the Ice Hotel.

CONVERSATION

A. _Listen to the conversation. Then listen again and repeat._

Sami: My friends and I are going to go ice-skating on a lake this weekend.

Jona: <u>You're kidding!</u> The most adventure you usually have is a trip to the movie theater.

Sami: <u>Actually</u>, you're wrong about that. Anyway, do you want to come with us or not?

Jona: Of course I want to go! <u>It's up to</u> my boss though. I may have to work this weekend.

Do you know these expressions? What do you think they mean?

You're kidding!   Actually   It's up to

B. *Work with a partner. Practice a part of the conversation. Replace the underlined words with the words below.*

Sami: My friends and I are going to go ice-skating on a lake this weekend.

Jona: <u>You're kidding</u>! The most adventure you usually have is a trip to the movie theater.

Are you serious?   You're joking!

C. Your Turn. *Write a new conversation. Use some of the words below and your own ideas. Practice the conversation with a partner.*

You're kidding!   Actually   It's up to

Go to page 153 for the Internet Activity.

<table>
<tr>
<td>

DID YOU KNOW?

</td>
<td>

- Norway has the world's largest population of Arctic reindeer.
- Sweden invented and perfected many things, such as the zipper, the refrigerator, and the computer mouse.
- In Denmark, people put a flag outside their house on their birthday.

</td>
<td>

</td>
</tr>
</table>

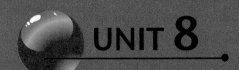

UNIT 8

WHAT ARE SOME UNUSUAL PLANTS?

Answer these questions.

1. What are some unusual plants around the world?

2. What are some plants that grow in your country but not in many others?

3. What is your favorite tree or plant?

MEANING

Listen to the talk. Then write the correct words in the blanks.

| bud | continuously | endangered | leaves |
| collectors | doubt | flowers | roots |

1. I am certain that my answer is correct. I have no _____ at all.

2. The flat green parts that grow on a plant are its _____.

3. Some animals are _____ because there are very few left in the world.

4. The _____ of a plant go down into the ground.

5. Some people are _____ of unusual plants.

6. My rose plant has a new _____ on it.

7. The garden is full of colorful _____.

8. You have to care for houseplants _____ to keep them alive.

WORDS THAT GO TOGETHER

Write the correct words in the blanks.

| doing research on | harsh conditions | morning dew |

1. We are having _____ this winter because of the many snow storms and cold weather.

2. Every day I study and look for information on mangrove trees because I'm _____ them.

3. At sunrise, the plants in my garden look wet because there is _____ on them.

USE

Work with a partner to answer the questions. Use complete sentences.

1. What is a way to find the truth about something we *doubt*?

2. Where is a place that has *harsh conditions* for living?

3. What is something you do *continuously*?

(continued)

4. What is your favorite *flower*?

5. What is the job of the *roots* of a plant?

6. Why are plant *leaves* important to us?

7. What are some things that are popular with *collectors*?

8. What animal or plant do you know that is *endangered*?

COMPREHENSION: LONG TALK

UNDERSTANDING THE LISTENING

Listen to the talk. Then circle the letter of the correct answer.

1. What is unusual about the Southeast Asian plant that the student is doing research on?

   a. where it grows

   b. how long it takes to grow flowers

   c. how quickly it grows flowers

2. What does the student say about the Welwitschia plant?

   a. It survives many years in the harsh conditions of the desert.

   b. It's a very small plant that survives in the desert.

   c. It has many leaves that get water from the morning dew.

3. What can the Saguaro cactus do?

   a. hold a lot of water inside it

   b. live anywhere

   c. grow up to 200 feet tall

REMEMBERING DETAILS

Listen to the talk again. Then answer these questions.

1. How long can the unusual Southeast Asian plant have fruit?

2. Where does the Welwitschia plant get its water from?

3. Why is the Welwitschia plant endangered?

4. Where does the Saguaro cactus grow?

5. Where does the biggest flower in the world grow?

6. How long does the biggest flower in the world live?

TAKING NOTES: Plants

 Listen and write notes about the description. Which plant does it describe?

Welwitschia plant

Saguaro cactus

COMPREHENSION: SHORT CONVERSATIONS

Listen to the conversations. Then circle the letter of the correct answer.

CONVERSATION 1

1. What does the woman want?

   a. to have flowers for herself

   b. to win a prize for her flowers

   c. to no longer care for her garden

CONVERSATION 2

2. Who is the man talking to?

   a. a collector

   b. a friend

   c. a shopkeeper

CONVERSATION 3

3. Why is the man sad?

   a. He doesn't have many plants in his collection.

   b. His plant is very old.

   c. His plant is endangered.

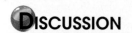

DISCUSSION

Discuss the answers to these questions with your classmates.

1. Why are deserts a hard place for plants to live? What are some other harsh conditions for plants?
2. What are some kinds of plants that grow in the following areas: tropical forests, mountains, deserts, plains? What places do you think have the most beautiful plants? Why?
3. What areas in your country are good for plants to grow? In what areas are the conditions harsh for plants? Do you like to grow flowers and plants? Why or why not?

CRITICAL THINKING

Work with a partner. Ask each other the following questions. Discuss your answers.

1. Besides being beautiful or interesting, what do plants give us? Why is it important to protect endangered plants? Why is it important to protect forests, especially tropical forests? What can nations and individuals do to help protect plants and trees?
2. Would you like to do research on unusual plants? Why or why not? What kind of research interests you? Why?

LANGUAGE FOCUS

CAN FOR ABILITY

Statements	Questions and Answers
I/You/He/She/It/We/You/They **can** live here. I/You/He/She/It/We/You/They **can't (cannot)** live here.	Q: **Can** I/you/he/she/it/we/you/they **live here**? A: Yes, I/you/he/she/it/we/you/they **can**. No, I/you/he/she/it/we/you/they **can't (cannot)**.

We use *can* to talk about ability in the present.

> *The plant can grow in the desert.*
> *It can't grow in a tropical forest.*

A. *Complete each sentence with* can *or* can't.

1. Nothing _____ survive here. It's too cold!

2. Be careful! Don't water it too much. It _____ die.

3. A rose bush _____ live in the desert.

4. Don't kill the roots! This tree _____ live without roots.

5. It's nice to have a plant that _____ grow flowers all year.

6. You _____ cut the flowers in public gardens.

B. *Work with a partner. Say what you can and can't do. Use the words below or your own words.*

| write with both hands | ski | dance | speak two languages | sing |

run five miles   play the guitar

PRONUNCIATION

CAN AND *CAN'T*

A. *Listen and notice the sound of* can *and* can't. *Then listen again and repeat.*

1. It can grow here.
2. It can't grow here.
3. They can survive.
4. They can't survive.

B. *Listen. Then write the correct words in the blanks.*

1. I _____ see it.

2. It _____ grow here.

3. You _____ cut it.

4. They _____ grow flowers.

5. You _____ plant it.

6. She _____ plant it here.

CONVERSATION

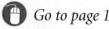 **A.** *Listen to the conversation. Then listen again and repeat.*

> **Lisa:** We're so high up on this mountain and there are still so many plants around us. I think these are very harsh conditions for plants!
>
> **Carlos:** Me, too. <u>I can't believe it!</u> <u>By the way</u>, I think you're a very good climber.
>
> **Lisa:** Thanks. Well, I think it's time to go. It's getting late.
>
> **Carlos:** <u>What a shame!</u> I'm not ready to leave!

Do you know these expressions? What do you think they mean?

| I can't believe it! | By the way | What a shame! |

B. *Work with a partner. Practice a part of the conversation. Replace the underlined words with the words below.*

> **Lisa:** We're so high up on this mountain and there are still so many plants around us. I think these are very harsh conditions for plants!
>
> **Carlos:** Me, too. <u>I can't believe it!</u> By the way, I think you're a very good climber.

| It's unbelievable! | It's incredible! |

C. Your Turn. *Write a new conversation. Use some of the words below and your own ideas. Practice the conversation with a partner.*

| I can't believe it! | By the way | What a shame! |

 Go to page 153 for the Internet Activity.

| **DID YOU KNOW?** | • The world's oldest tree is a bristlecone pine in California. It's close to 5,000 years old.
• An olive tree can live for up to 1,500 years.
• The Venus flytrap, a plant that eats insects, can live without eating for more than a month. | |

WHAT ARE SOME FAMOUS STRUCTURES AROUND THE WORLD?

before you listen

Answer these questions.

1. What is a famous structure in your country?

2. What are some famous structures around the world?

3. Where are some of the tallest buildings in the world?

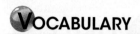

VOCABULARY

MEANING

Listen to the talk. Then write the correct words in the blanks.

brave	frame	iron	monument
competition	invention	landmarks	success

1. The Internet is an ___invention___ from the 1960s.

2. There are four teams in the ___competition___ to design a new building, and they all want to win.

3. You know you're in New York when you see famous ___landmarks___ like the Empire State Building.

4. A ___brave___ person shows courage during times of danger or difficulty.

5. The Statue of Liberty is a famous ___monument___ that is a symbol of freedom.

6. You need to build a ___frame___ for a house before you put up the walls and roof.

7. The design for the new building is a ___success___ —all of the designers like it.

8. ___Iron___ is a heavy, strong metal that people use to make tools and build things.

WORDS THAT GO TOGETHER

Write the correct words in the blanks.

a symbol of	comes from	get a medal

1. The winners of the race ___get a medal___ that is gold and has words and pictures on it.

2. His good health ___comes from___ his efforts to eat well and exercise.

3. A dove is ___a symbol of___ peace in many places around the world.

USE

Work with a partner to answer the questions. Use complete sentences.

1. What are some famous _landmarks_ in your city or country?

2. Where is there a _monument_ where you live?

3. What is your favorite *invention*? افتراع
4. Who do you think is a *brave* person? شجاع
5. What do you have that is *a symbol of* something? رمز
6. What is an event at which athletes *get a medal*?
7. What do builders usually use to make a *frame* for a house?
8. What is fun about a *competition*? متنافس

COMPREHENSION: LONG TALK

UNDERSTANDING THE LISTENING

Listen to the talk. Then circle the letter of the correct answer.

1. What did Gustave Eiffel do before he designed the Eiffel Tower?

   a. He designed a new kind of bridge.
   b. He moved to New York.
   c. He sailed through the Panama Canal.

2. Why did Gustave Eiffel design the Eiffel Tower?

   a. to win a competition
   b. to make a monument for Paris
   c. to get to the World's Fair

3. What did Parisians think of the tower?

   a. They admired it.
   b. They enjoyed going to the top of it.
   c. They disliked it.

REMEMBERING DETAILS

Listen to the talk again. Circle T if the sentence is true. Circle F if the sentence is false.

1. Gustave Eiffel designed a stone bridge.	T	**F**
2. Gustave Eiffel designed gates for a canal.	**T**	F
3. It took three years to build the Eiffel Tower.	T	**F**
4. The Eiffel Tower was the tallest building at the time.	**T**	F
5. People used a staircase to get to the top of the tower.	T	**F**
6. People who went to the top of the tower received tickets to the World's Fair.	T	**F**

TAKING NOTES: Structures

🎧 *Listen and write notes about the description. Which structure does it describe?*

**Sydney Opera House,
Australia**

Colosseum, Italy

COMPREHENSION: SHORT CONVERSATIONS

🎧 *Listen to the conversations. Then circle the letter of the correct answer.*

CONVERSATION 1

1. What did the woman see on the last day of her trip?

   a. Chinatown   **b.** Alcatraz   **c.** the Golden Gate Bridge

CONVERSATION 2

2. Why is the man unhappy?

   a. The weather is too bad to see London's landmarks.   **b.** He's too tired to see London's landmarks.   **c.** He doesn't have time to see London's landmarks.

CONVERSATION 3

3. What does the man want to do in Australia?

   a. see the Sydney Opera House   **b.** swim at the Barrier Reef   **c.** hike in the outback

DISCUSSION

Discuss the answers to these questions with your classmates.

1. What landmark or monument did you visit in the past? Did you enjoy it? Why or why not? What landmark or monument do you want to visit in the future? Why?

2. What are some structures, monuments, or places that are symbols of the area they are in? What do they say about the place or people there?

3. How brave are you? Do you like to go to the tops of tall buildings or other high places? Why or why not? What kinds of places make you feel uncomfortable? What kinds of places do you like? Why?

CRITICAL THINKING

Work with a partner. Ask each other the following questions. Discuss your answers.

1. The Parisians disliked the Eiffel Tower after Gustave Eiffel designed it. People often don't like the designs of new buildings. Why do you think they feel that way? Is this true of other products and inventions, too? Why are people not always eager, or ready and willing, to accept new things in their lives?
2. Imagine you are a designer. Choose a city, area, or country and create a monument for it. What does it look like? What is it made from? How is it a symbol of the area or people there?

LANGUAGE FOCUS

SIMPLE PAST

<table>
<tr><th colspan="3">REGULAR VERBS</th></tr>
<tr><th>Verb Endings</th><th>Base Form</th><th>Simple Past</th></tr>
<tr><td>Add -ed (most verbs)</td><td>need
work</td><td>needed
worked</td></tr>
<tr><td>Add -d (verbs ending in -e)</td><td>live</td><td>lived</td></tr>
<tr><td>Add -ied (verbs ending in consonant + y)</td><td>study</td><td>studied</td></tr>
</table>

<table>
<tr><th colspan="4">IRREGULAR VERBS</th></tr>
<tr><th>Base Form</th><th>Simple Past</th><th>Base Form</th><th>Simple Past</th></tr>
<tr><td>be</td><td>was</td><td>become</td><td>became</td></tr>
<tr><td>have</td><td>had</td><td>see</td><td>saw</td></tr>
<tr><td>get</td><td>got</td><td>take</td><td>took</td></tr>
<tr><td>go</td><td>went</td><td>think</td><td>thought</td></tr>
<tr><td>begin</td><td>began</td><td>stand</td><td>stood</td></tr>
</table>

The **simple past** is the same for all personal pronouns (*I, you, he, she, it, we,* and *they*). We use the simple past

- for actions and situations that began and ended in the past.
- with time expressions like *yesterday, last week,* and *ago.*

A. *Complete the paragraph with the simple past of the verbs.*

The French _wanted_ to give a gift to celebrate the freedom of the Americans. They
  1. (want)

decided to give a statue. The French people _collected_ money for the statue and
2. (decide)   3. (collect)

started to build it. The designers _were_ Auguste Bartholdi and Gustave Eiffel.
4. (start)   5. (be)

They _designed_ the frame of the statue. They _completed_ the statue in 1884, but they
    6. (design)   7. (complete)

took the statue apart to ship it to New York because it was so big. In 1886, the Statue
8. (take)

of Liberty _stood_ on Liberty Island and it _became_ a big attraction.
      9. (stand)   10. (become)

B. *Work with a partner. Tell each other four things you did before you arrived to class today.*

PRONUNCIATION

THE PAST -*ED* ENDING

A. *Listen and notice the sound of the past -ed ending. Then listen again and repeat.*

/d/	/t/	/ɪd/
1. lived	4. worked	7. wanted
2. designed	5. liked	8. visited
3. entered	6. helped	9. started

B. *Listen to the words. Check the box for the final -ed sound you hear.*

	/d/	/t/	/ɪd/
1. covered	X		
2. collected			X
3. owned	X		
4. completed			X
5. watched		X	
6. walked		X	

 A. *Listen to the conversation. Then listen again and repeat.*

Amanda: When you were in New York, did you go to the top of the Statue of Liberty?

John: Yes, but I was a bit scared up there. <u>Eventually</u>, I got used to it though.

Amanda: I totally understand! I didn't even visit the Eiffel Tower when I was in Paris. <u>At the time</u>, I was afraid of elevators.

John: Really? Well, <u>I promise you</u>, the view from the Eiffel Tower is incredible!

Do you know these expressions? What do you think they mean?

> Eventually   At the time   I promise you

B. *Work with a partner. Practice a part of the conversation. Replace the underlined words with the words below.*

Amanda: When you were in New York, did you go to the top of the Statue of Liberty?

John: Yes, but I was a bit scared up there. <u>Eventually</u>, I got used to it though.

> After a while   Finally

C. Your Turn. *Write a new conversation. Use some of the words below and your own ideas. Practice the conversation with a partner.*

> Eventually   At the time   I promise you

Go to page 154 for the Internet Activity.

DID YOU KNOW?	• Workers repaint the Eiffel Tower every seven years. • The Great Pyramid in Egypt was 482 feet tall, but over time, the weather and the sinking of the Earth made it 30 feet shorter. • The Panama Canal took thirty-four years to build. About 80,000 people died during its construction, mostly from disease.	

WHAT KINDS OF BAD WEATHER ARE THERE?

before you listen

Answer these questions.

1. What kinds of bad weather are there in your country?

2. What areas of the world have bad weather related to wind or rain?

3. What kind of weather do you like the least?

VOCABULARY

MEANING

🎧 *Listen to the talk. Then write the correct words in the blanks.*

alternate	destructive	remove	storm
committee	list	replaced	upset

1. There is going to be a __strom__ with strong winds and rain.

2. I'm going to __remove__ that sign from the house so it doesn't blow away.

3. The group of people on the __committee__ decided how much money to spend to protect the buildings from bad weather.

4. The winds were very __destructive__ because they caused harm to people and damaged buildings.

5. I have a __list__ of all the things I need to do before the cold weather comes.

6. Martha was __upset__ when it rained on her birthday.

7. We __alternate__ houses—in the winter we live in Florida and in the summer we live in New York.

8. A tree fell on our roof, so we __replaced__ the roof with a new one.

WORDS THAT GO TOGETHER

Write the correct words in the blanks.

alphabetical order	named after	weather service

1. Scientists at the __weather service__ study the clouds, sky, winds, and other conditions.

2. I have the names of the countries I visited in __alphabetical order__, starting with Australia under the letter "A."

3. The building is __named after__ a famous architect.

USE

Work with a partner to answer the questions. Use complete sentences.

1. Where are there many *destructive* storms?
2. What place do you know that is *named after* a famous person?
3. Why do people put names in *alphabetical order*?
4. When does the weather make you *upset*?
5. What happens during a *storm*?
6. When do you make a *list*?
7. What does the *weather service* tell us?
8. Why do we sometimes need a *committee*?

COMPREHENSION: LONG TALK

UNDERSTANDING THE LISTENING

Listen to the talk. Then circle the letter of the correct answer.

1. Why did countries start to give names to hurricanes?

   a. It's an easy way to remember different storms.

   b. Weather service scientists wanted to use their names for storms.

   c. A committee decided the storms were as dangerous as some people.

2. How do hurricanes get their names?

   a. Famous people name them.

   b. A committee uses several lists of names.

   c. The weather service has names for all of the different kinds of storms.

3. How do people give names to hurricanes in the Atlantic and Pacific Oceans?

   a. They choose names from the same list.

   b. They use English names for the Atlantic Ocean and Spanish names for the Pacific Ocean.

   c. They choose names from two different lists.

REMEMBERING DETAILS

Listen to the talk again. Then answer these questions.

1. Why did some countries start to give hurricanes different names?
2. Who were the first hurricanes named after?
3. How many lists of names are there?
4. Which letters are NOT on the lists?
5. When do they remove a name from the lists?
6. What kinds of names do the hurricanes that happen near the Atlantic Ocean have?

TAKING NOTES: Storms

Listen and write notes about the description. Which kind of storm does it describe?

dust storm

thunderstorm

COMPREHENSION: SHORT CONVERSATIONS

Listen to the conversations. Then circle the letter of the correct answer.

CONVERSATION 1

1. What does the woman think about the tree names?

   a. She thinks they're strange.

   b. She thinks they're a good idea.

   c. She thinks they're going to make the trees famous.

CONVERSATION 2

2. Who is the woman talking to?

   a. her travel agent

   b. the weather service

   c. a tour guide

CONVERSATION 3

3. How does the man feel about the hot weather?

   a. angry

   b. tired

   c. pleased

DISCUSSION

Discuss the answers to these questions with your classmates.

1. What countries or areas of the world have the best weather? What are some nice places to live because of the weather there?

2. Do you think it's a good idea to name storms? Why or why not? Why do you think the committee removes the names of destructive storms from the list? What other things in nature do people give names to? What man-made things do people give names to?

3. What kind of destruction can hurricanes cause? What are some other dangerous kinds of weather?

CRITICAL THINKING

Work with a partner. Ask each other the following questions. Discuss your answers.

1. What is your favorite kind of weather? Why? Imagine you can control the weather. What is the weather like in your perfect place? Are there seasons? Are there changes in the weather?

2. What are natural disasters? Give some examples of recent natural disasters. How do people around the world help others who suffer from natural disasters? What can governments do to help? What can ordinary people do?

LANGUAGE FOCUS

ALL OF THE/EVERY

- We can use a plural count or non-count noun after these expressions: *all of the, some of the, none of the.*
- The verb can be singular or plural. The noun tells us which one to use.

  All of the names were female. (*names* is plural, so verb is plural)
  Some of the storms were very destructive. (*storms* is plural, so verb is plural)
  None of the wind was in this area. (*wind* is singular, so verb is singular)

- *Every* means "all." We use *every* with a singular count noun and a singular verb.

  Every day was sunny and warm.

A. *Circle the correct verb that completes each sentence.*

1. Every hurricane (have / has) a name.
2. Every season (have / has) a new list of names.
3. In the beginning, all of the names (was / were) female names.
4. Every name (start / starts) with a different letter.
5. In the beginning, none of the names (was / were) male names.
6. Some of the names (do / does) not appear on the list again.

B. *Work with a partner. Think of five sentences using* all of the, some of the, none of the, *and* every. *Use each phrase or word at least once.*

PRONUNCIATION

QUESTION INTONATION

 A. *Listen to the questions. Notice the intonation of the* Yes/No *questions and the* Wh-*questions. The intonation goes up at the end of* Yes/No *questions and down at the end of* Wh- *questions. Then listen again and repeat.*

Yes/No Questions

1. Is that a question? ↑
2. Are there any questions? ↑

Wh- Questions

3. Why do they have names? ↓
4. What letter is that? ↓

 B. *Listen. Then write the intonation you hear:* ↑ *or* ↓.

1. What is happening? [ ]
2. Is the storm dangerous? [ ]
3. Are all the names English? [ ]
4. What are they doing? [ ]
5. When is it coming this way? [ ]
6. Are they warning us? [ ]

CONVERSATION

 A. *Listen to the conversation. Then listen again and repeat.*

>   **Sasha:** <u>Do you mind</u> if I sit here?
>   **Martin:** <u>Not at all.</u> I'm so glad this is our last class of the week!
>   **Sasha:** Me, too! By the way, are you going to the lake again this weekend?
>   **Martin:** It depends on the weather. <u>Naturally</u>, I don't want to go there if it's raining.

Do you know these expressions? What do you think they mean?

Do you mind   **Not at all.**   **Naturally**

B. *Work with a partner. Practice a part of the conversation. Replace the underlined words with the words below.*

>   **Sasha:** Do you mind if I sit here?
>   **Martin:** <u>Not at all.</u> I'm so glad this is our last class of the week!

Of course not.   **Please do.**

C. Your Turn. *Write a new conversation. Use some of the words below and your own ideas. Practice the conversation with a partner.*

Do you mind   **Not at all.**   **Naturally**

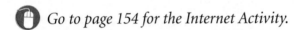 *Go to page 154 for the Internet Activity.*

| **DID YOU KNOW?** | <ul><li>Lightning does good, too. It puts nitrogen into the soil. Plants need nitrogen to survive.</li><li>Whirlwinds or dust devils usually carry sand and dirt, but they can also suck fire from a forest fire and carry its flames.</li><li>There are about 2,000 thunderstorms around the world each minute.</li></ul> |  |

A. COMPREHENSION

Circle the letter of the correct answer.

1. The difference between non-fiction and fiction books is _____.

   a. one is about things that are not real while the other is about facts

   b. one has a hard cover while the other has a soft paper cover

   c. one is a file in your computer while the other is a book that you can hold

   d. one is about adventure and romance while the other has cartoons in it

2. In Japan, to give and receive *nengajo* cards is _____.

   a. no longer important

   b. an exciting part of New Year's Day

   c. mostly for children

   d. a part of family celebrations only

3. The White House is _____.

   a. where the U.S. president lives and works

   b. the place where U.S. lawmakers meet to pass the nation's laws

   c. a famous U.S. building that tourists visit but no one lives there

   d. a private home for the U.S. president's family that no one else can see or visit

4. For Hindus in India, cows are very important because they _____.

   a. are good pets

   b. take the place of cars

   c. are worth a lot of money when the owners sell them

   d. provide food and labor

5. Gift giving _____.

   a. is not appropriate in any cultures

   b. is something you never have to worry about doing wrong

   c. changes according to cultures and occasions

   d. is something a person should not do outside of the family

6. Kimchi _____.
   a. is not popular everywhere in Korea
   b. is the name of a dish with many different kinds of meats
   c. has different tastes according to who, where, and when people make it
   d. doesn't have much flavor because it has few spices

7. The Ice Hotel _____.
   a. has its name because of the cold area it's in
   b. is a structure that is so old that it has ice all over it
   c. isn't really a hotel where people can stay, but a beautiful sculpture that tourists go to see
   d. is a structure that designers and sculptors make from tons of ice every year

8. The woman talks about some plants that are unusual because of _____.
   a. their beauty
   b. where and how long they grow
   c. the food they provide
   d. why people want to collect them

9. The purpose of the Eiffel Tower was to _____.
   a. make Paris the home of the tallest building in the world
   b. be a landmark for a World's Fair in Paris
   c. make Gustave Eiffel famous
   d. test a new elevator by the Otis Elevator Company

10. The weather service gives names to storms according to _____.
    a. their alphabetical order on a group of lists
    b. how strong or destructive the storms are
    c. where and what time of year the storms take place
    d. a list of the most famous storms of the past

B. VOCABULARY

Circle the letter of the correct answer.

1. Any book which has a soft cover is a _____ book.

    a. hardcover   **b.** fiction   **c.** paperback   **d.** nonfiction

2. People put letters they want to send into _____ on the street.

    a. mailboxes   **b.** electronics   **c.** eBooks   **d.** novels

3. To get to higher floors in a building, people walk up and down _____.

    a. elevators   **b.** staircases   **c.** novels   **d.** series

4. Large vehicles with big wheels that help farmers work in the fields are called _____.

    a. elevators   **b.** drapes   **c.** utensils   **d.** tractors

5. An important event or celebration is _____.

    a. an occasion   **b.** a present   **c.** an oval   **d.** a lawn

6. A list of ingredients and instructions that tell you how to cook something is called a _____.

    a. region   **b.** recipe   **c.** host   **d.** collection

7. Something that looks large and important is _____.

    a. grand   **b.** unique   **c.** appropriate   **d.** sacred

8. The drops of water on plants that form during the night are _____.

    a. below freezing   **b.** in season   **c.** morning dew   **d.** harsh conditions

9. The main pieces of material that hold up a building make up its _____.

    a. monument   **b.** roots   **c.** landmark   **d.** frame

10. Scientists study the sky, clouds, winds, and other conditions at _____.

    a. modern times   **b.** the weather service   **c.** harsh conditions   **d.** the postal service

C. LANGUAGE FOCUS

Circle the letter of the correct answer.

1. My brother _____ twenty years old.

   a. is   **b.** has   **c.** have   **d.** be

2. I _____ my New Year's cards now.

   a. writing   **b.** write   **c.** am writing   **d.** is writing

3. She _____ with her mother any more.

   a. not live   **b.** doesn't live   **c.** doesn't lives   **d.** no live

4. He _____ fruits and vegetables.

   a. eat usually   **b.** is usually eat   **c.** usually eat   **d.** usually eats

5. A gift of flowers is _____ than a vase.

   a. more suitabler   **b.** suitabler   **c.** more suitable   **d.** suitable

6. I don't have _____.

   a. any garlic   **b.** some garlic   **c.** some garlics   **d.** any garlics

7. He _____ visit Sweden next year.

   a. not going to   **b.** isn't going to   **c.** isn't going   **d.** isn't be going to

8. This plant _____ here.

   a. can't to survive   **b.** can't survives   **c.** can't be survive   **d.** can't survive

9. In 1891, most Parisians _____ the Eiffel Tower was ugly.

   a. thinked   **b.** thank   **c.** thought   **d.** think

10. _____ hurricane has a male or female first name.

    a. All of the   **b.** Some   **c.** Any   **d.** Every

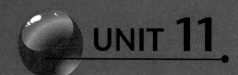

WHO ARE SOME FAMOUS PHILANTHROPISTS?

Answer these questions.

1. Who are some famous rich people you know who help others?

2. Who are some people who are not rich and help others?

3. What do you do to help others?

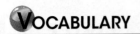

MEANING

🎧 *Listen to the talk. Then write the correct words in the blanks.*

camp	donated	illness	philanthropy
charity	generous	kindness	profits

1. We give money to a _____ that helps the poor.

2. Some people show _____ to others by helping and caring about them.

3. The man is in very bad health because of his _____.

4. Many rich people are very _____ with their money.

5. We're going to sell old clothes and use the _____ to buy food for people who are hungry.

6. Julio _____ clothing to children who don't have a home.

7. Victor gives money and help to others, and they live better lives because of his _____.

8. I teach at a _____ in the summer that gives kids from cities the opportunity to experience nature.

WORDS THAT GO TOGETHER

Write the correct words in the blanks.

make a difference	salad dressings	to forget about

1. We have two different _____ to put on our lettuce.

2. When people _____, they change things and make life better for others.

3. It's important to remember and not _____ people who are kind to us.

USE

Work with a partner to answer the questions. Use complete sentences.

1. What have you *donated*?
2. What is special about going to *camp*?
3. What kind of *salad dressings* do you like?
4. Who do you know that is *generous*?
5. What is the name of a *charity* that you know about?
6. How do we know when we have an *illness*?
7. Who is someone who *makes a difference* because of what he or she does for others?
8. How does a person show *kindness*?

COMPREHENSION: LONG TALK

UNDERSTANDING THE LISTENING

Listen to the talk. Then circle the letter of the correct answer.

1. What did Paul Newman think about his success?
    a. He didn't like it.
    b. He knew it made him better than others.
    c. He wanted to use it to help others.

2. Why did Paul Newman start the company Newman's Own?
    a. A friend told him to do it.
    b. He wanted to make more money.
    c. He wanted to help people.

3. Who did Newman start the Hole in the Wall Gang Camp for?
    a. a group of actors
    b. poor people
    c. sick children

REMEMBERING DETAILS

Listen to the talk again. Circle T if the sentence is true. Circle F if the sentence is false.

1. Paul Newman believed that his success came from his hard work.

    T   F

2. Paul Newman didn't like to cook.

    T   F

3. When Paul Newman started Newman's Own, it was a big joke to him.

    T   F

(continued)

4. Newman's Own is a company that sells clothes.   T   F

5. Newman's Own gives 50 percent of its profits to charity.   T   F

6. The name of the Hole in the Wall Gang Camp came   T   F
   from a movie.

TAKING NOTES: Philanthropists

🎧 *Listen and write notes about the description. Which philanthropist does it describe?*

*Andrew Carnegie made
his money from steel.*

*John D. Rockefeller made
his money from oil.*

COMPREHENSION: SHORT CONVERSATIONS

🎧 *Listen to the conversations. Then circle the letter of the correct answer.*

CONVERSATION 1

1. Where is the woman?

   a. at a hospital   **b.** at a dance   **c.** in a shop

CONVERSATION 2

2. Why is the woman upset with the man?

   a. He gave her clothes   **b.** He cleaned her   **c.** He put her
   to charity.   clothes by   clothes in bags.
                                     mistake.

CONVERSATION 3

3. Which camp is the best place for swimming?

   a. Little Rock   **b.** Big Tree   **c.** Big Mountain

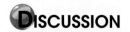

DISCUSSION

Discuss the answers to these questions with your classmates.

1. What are some international groups that help people? What kind of help do they give?
2. What are some ways that ordinary people can help others?
3. Who are some people that need help around the world?

CRITICAL THINKING

Work with a partner. Ask each other the following questions. Discuss your answers.

1. Do you think rich people and big companies have a duty, or a responsibility, to share their wealth and help others? Why or why not?
2. Imagine you are very wealthy, or rich. Do you use your wealth to help others? In what ways? What are the best ways to help people? What do people need most? Is help always good? Are there times when helping someone isn't the best thing to do? Explain.

LANGUAGE FOCUS

SUPERLATIVES OF ADJECTIVES

Adjective Descriptions	Adjectives	Superlatives
short adjectives (1 syllable)	rich	the richest
adjectives ending in -*y*	lucky	the luckiest
long adjectives (2 or more syllables)	successful	the most successful
irregular adjectives	good bad	the best the worst

- We use comparatives of adjectives to compare two people, places, or things.
- We use **superlatives of adjectives** to compare one person, place, or thing to two or more people, places, or things.

A. *Complete the sentences with the superlative form of the adjectives.*

1. They have (good) _____ camps for children.
2. He was (great) _____ philanthropist I know.
3. He was (kind) _____ man I know.
4. She said she was (lucky) _____ person in the world.
5. She was (generous) _____ woman.
6. I think she was (beautiful) _____ woman.

B. *Work with a partner. Ask each other the following questions: Who is the wealthiest person in your country? Who is the most famous movie star? Who is the most generous person? What is the poorest area? Use complete sentences to answer.*

PRONUNCIATION

VOWEL SOUNDS: *rich* /ɪ/, *reach* /i/

A. *Listen and repeat. Underline the word with a different sound in each group.*

1. rich   bin   hill   seal
2. cheap   sheep   pill   heel

B. *Work with a partner. Say the words below. Then write them in the correct column of the chart.*

meat   wish   Tim   film   ill   meal   bean   cheek   chick   teach

/ɪ/	/i/

CONVERSATION

A. *Listen to the conversation. Then listen again and repeat.*

Nora: John is a kind man but he's never going to be successful.

Lee: <u>I'm afraid</u> you're right. He thinks everything is <u>a big joke</u>.

Nora: But look at you. You're the best teacher I know.

Lee: Well, <u>I'm just lucky</u>, I guess. I'm doing something I love.

Do you know these expressions? What do you think they mean?

I'm afraid   a big joke   I'm just lucky

B. *Work with a partner. Practice a part of the conversation. Replace the underlined words with the words below.*

Nora: You know, John is a kind man but he's never going to be successful.

Lee: I'm afraid you're right. He thinks everything is <u>a big joke</u>.

funny   something to laugh about

C. Your Turn. *Write a new conversation. Use some of the words below and your own ideas. Practice the conversation with a partner.*

I'm afraid   a big joke   I'm just lucky

 Go to page 154 for the Internet Activity.

DID YOU KNOW?	• The Bill Gates Foundation is one of the world's largest charities. • Andrew Carnegie built 2,507 libraries in the United States and around the world. • Oprah Winfrey is one of the celebrities that donates the most money to charities.	

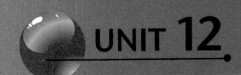
WHAT DO YOU KNOW ABOUT DESERTS?

before you listen

Answer these questions.

1. What are some famous deserts around the world?

2. What does a desert look like?

3. What is the weather like in a desert?

VOCABULARY

MEANING

🎧 *Listen to the talk. Then write the correct words in the blanks.*

consider تأمل	environment بيئة	floods فيضانات	rocky صخري
drown يغرق	extreme اقصى	pour يسكب	sand رمل

1. The people, plants, and animals around us are all part of the __environment__ in which we live.

2. Look at those clouds! It's going to __pour__ rain.

3. We are having __extreme__ weather. It's very hot one day and very cold the next.

4. It's raining so hard and the rivers are so high that I'm afraid there will be __floods__.

5. We need to think about and __consider__ everything before we decide where to travel.

6. This __rocky__ ground has many stones on it, so be careful where you walk.

7. Some people __drown__ when they go into the water and can't swim.

8. I like to walk without shoes and feel the __sand__ under my feet at the beach.

WORDS THAT GO TOGETHER

Write the correct words in the blanks.

definition of المعاني من	die of thirst الموت من العطش	tropical forests الغابات الاستوائية

1. Those cows will __die of thirst__ if they don't drink some water very soon.

2. When I don't know the meaning of a word, I ask my teacher to give me the __definition of__ it.

3. __tropical forests__ are warm and wet, and have many different kinds of trees.

USE

Work with a partner to answer the questions. Use complete sentences.

1. What happens during *floods*?
2. What is something you *consider* before you plan a trip?
3. What kind of *environment* do polar bears live in?
4. Where are there *tropical forests*?
5. Where do you find the *definition of* a word?
6. What is a place that has *extreme* weather conditions?
7. What is something that you *pour*?
8. Where does *sand* come from?

COMPREHENSION: LONG TALK

UNDERSTANDING THE LISTENING

Listen to the talk. Then circle the letter of the correct answer.

1. What is a desert?

    a. a place with rocks and sand
    b. a place where there is little rain
    c. a place where it is always hot

2. Which statement is true?

    a. It never rains in the desert.
    b. It rains a little, then it stops.
    c. When it rains in the desert, it pours.

3. Why do deserts sometimes have scary names?

    a. There's no life in the desert.
    b. It's hard to survive the conditions there.
    c. Extremely dangerous animals live there.

REMEMBERING DETAILS

Listen to the talk again. Then write the correct words in the blanks.

1. Earth is _____20%_____ percent desert.
2. Some people consider Antarctica a desert because it has no _____rain_____.
3. Many people say that the _____Sahara_____ is the world's largest desert.

4. It's more common to ___drow___ in the desert than it is to die of thirst.

5. Many deserts are ___rocky___ and have little sand.

6. The Gobi Desert is in ___Mongolia___.

TAKING NOTES: Deserts

Listen and write notes about the description. Which desert does it describe?

Gobi Desert, Mongolia

Death Valley, United States

COMPREHENSION: SHORT CONVERSATIONS

Listen to the conversations. Then circle the letter of the correct answer.

CONVERSATION 1

1. Where is the woman probably going to go on vacation?

   a. to the mountains

   b. to the Sahara Desert

   c. to a tropical forest

CONVERSATION 2

2. What is the man worried about?

   a. being lost

   b. not having enough water

   c. the heat

CONVERSATION 3

3. What is the woman going to do tonight?

   a. go to the talk

   b. work on her term paper

   c. work at the store

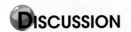

DISCUSSION

Discuss the answers to these questions with your classmates.

1. What are some places in which people live in extreme conditions? What characteristics do the people have who live in these places? What are their lives like? Could you live in an environment like that? Why or why not?

2. Are there deserts in your country? What are some of the different environments in your country? What kind of environment do you live in? Do you like where you live? Would you like to live someplace else? Why or why not?

3. Some people love the desert and enjoy living there. What are some benefits of living in the desert? What are some difficulties? Would you like to live in the desert? Why or why not?

CRITICAL THINKING

Work with a partner. Ask each other the following questions. Discuss your answers.

1. Does it surprise you that the variety of plants and animals in the desert is second only to tropical forests? Why? What are some plants and animals that live in deserts? What are some plants and animals that live in tropical forests?

2. Imagine you are going to live in the desert. How do you prepare to live there? What clothes do you wear? What dangers do you face? How do you survive and protect yourself?

LANGUAGE FOCUS

FUTURE WITH *WILL*

Statements	Questions and Answers
I/He/She/It/We/You/They**'ll (will) go** to the desert. I/He/She/It/We/You/They **won't (will not) go** to the desert.	Q: **Will** I/he/she/it/we/you/they **go** to the desert? A: Yes, I/he/she/it/we/you/they**'ll (will) go** to the desert. No, I/he/she/it/we/you/they **won't (will not) go** to the desert.

- We use **will** or *be going to* (see Unit 7) for predictions, or what we think will happen in the future.

> - We use *be going to* for actions that we planned or already decided to do. We use *will* for actions we decide at the moment of speaking.
>
>   **A:** *I can't lift this.*
>   **B:** *Wait. I'll help you.*
>
> - *Will* is contracted to *'ll* in the positive and *won't* in the negative. We do not use contractions in affirmative short answers.
>
>   CORRECT: *Yes, he **will**.*
>   NOT CORRECT: *Yes, he'll.*

A. *Complete the sentences with* will *or the* be going to *form of the verb. Use contractions.*

1. **A:** _____ you (take) _____ photos in the desert with Jim this weekend?

   B: I don't know. I (call) _____ Jim right now.

2. **A:** Look at the sky. It's (rain) _____. I can't go now.

   B: Don't worry. I (give) _____ you my umbrella.

3. **A:** What _____ the temperature (be) _____ in the Mojave desert on Sunday during the day?

   B: I don't know. I (look) _____ it up right now on my computer and tell you.

B. *Work with a partner. Make six predictions about the future in 2050 using* will.

EXAMPLE: People will use deserts for farming.

PRONUNCIATION

STRESSED SYLLABLES

In English there are no easy rules to learn where to put the stress on a word. The best way is to listen and repeat.

A. *Listen and say each word. Notice the stressed syllable.*

1. Sa<u>ha</u>ra
2. <u>A</u>sia
3. <u>de</u>sert
4. <u>A</u>frica
5. <u>Chi</u>na
6. Ant<u>arc</u>tica

B. *Listen and repeat. Underline the stressed syllable in each word.*

1. environment
2. Amazon
3. America
4. Gobi
5. Atlantic
6. Arctic

CONVERSATION

A. *Listen to the conversation. Then listen again and repeat.*

Karen: I'll never finish this paper on Death Valley and the Gobi Desert. I'm going to fail this course!

Ali: Don't be silly. I'll help you. I visited Death Valley last year.

Karen: But what about the Gobi? I don't have time for both subjects.

Ali: Well, I'll tell you what. My friend Jack has great books on the Gobi Desert. I'll borrow them from him.

Do you know these expressions? What do you think they mean?

Don't be silly.   what about   I'll tell you what

B. *Work with a partner. Practice a part of the conversation. Replace the underlined words with the words below.*

Karen: I'll never finish this paper on Death Valley and the Gobi Desert. I'm going to fail this course!

Ali: Don't be silly. I'll help you. I visited Death Valley last year.

Don't worry.   Nonsense.

C. Your Turn. *Write a new conversation. Use some of the words below and your own ideas. Practice the conversation with a partner.*

Don't be silly.   what about   I'll tell you what

Go to page 155 for the Internet Activity.

DID YOU KNOW?

- Camels are not from the Sahara Desert. People brought them from Asia about 2,000 years ago.
- The Salar de Uyuni desert in Bolivia, South America, is the world's largest source of salt on land.
- In parts of the Atacama Desert in Chile, it never rains.

WHAT ARE SOME DIFFERENT KINDS OF HOUSES?

before

you listen

Answer these questions.

1. What are some different kinds of houses you know?

2. What kind of house do you live in?

3. What is the most popular style of house in your country?

VOCABULARY

MEANING

🎧 *Listen to the talk. Then write the correct words in the blanks.*

drops	guess	privacy	row
entire	peculiar	roof	stories

1. The houses were in a _____, one next to the other.

2. This part of the mountain _____ straight down to a river 100 feet below.

3. Yesterday we painted the _____ kitchen. Now it's all red.

4. I'm not sure which house my friend lives in, so I'm going to _____.

5. The strange color of that house makes it look _____.

6. The _____ that covers our house is very old.

7. We want to build our new house away from the others because we like our _____.

8. Our house is very big. It has four _____.

WORDS THAT GO TOGETHER

Write the correct words in the blanks.

in particular	looks like	side by side

1. My sister _____ our mother, but she has our father's hair color.

2. They build the houses _____, with very little space between them.

3. I like our whole house, but I like the windows _____.

USE

Work with a partner to answer the questions. Use complete sentences.

1. How many *stories* does your house have?

2. What is a *peculiar* color for a house?

3. Where do we find seats in a *row*?

4. Who in your family *looks like* you?

5. What do you like *in particular* about your best friend?

6. Where is someplace you go for *privacy*?

7. Who do you like to walk *side by side* with?

8. What helps you *guess* what the weather is going to be like?

COMPREHENSION: LONG TALK

UNDERSTANDING THE LISTENING

Listen to the talk. Then circle the letter of the correct answer.

1. What does a saltbox house look like?

   a. long and narrow, with one story

   b. square with two stories in front and one story in back

   c. square with one story

2. Why don't shotgun houses have windows on the side?

   a. They're too small.

   b. They're close together.

   c. They have doors instead.

3. Which of the following describes a shotgun house?

   a. a narrow house with rooms in a row

   b. a wide house with rooms side by side

   c. a square house with rooms on top of each other

REMEMBERING DETAILS

Listen to the talk again. Then answer these questions.

1. Where in the United States are there many saltbox houses?
2. What did the saltbox house get its name from?
3. What does the roof of a saltbox house look like?
4. Where in the United States are there many shotgun houses?
5. How do some people think the shotgun house got its name?
6. What is special about a mobile home?

TAKING NOTES: Houses

🎧 *Listen and write notes about the description. Which house does it describe?*

boat house

mobile home

COMPREHENSION: SHORT CONVERSATIONS

🎧 *Listen to the conversations. Then circle the letter of the correct answer.*

CONVERSATION 1

1. When can the man see the mobile home?

   a. Wednesday   **b.** Thursday   **c.** Sunday

CONVERSATION 2

2. Where does the woman prefer to live?

   a. the countryside   **b.** the city   **c.** the coast

CONVERSATION 3

3. What does the man want the most in a new house?

   a. three bedrooms   **b.** two stories   **c.** one story

DISCUSSION

Discuss the answers to these questions with your classmates.

1. In your country, what is the difference between old house styles and new house styles?
2. What are the advantages and disadvantages of living in the following kinds of houses: small, large, one story, two stories?
3. Which do you prefer, a house or an apartment? Why? What are the advantages and disadvantages of each?

CRITICAL THINKING

Work with a partner. Ask each other the following questions. Discuss your answers.

1. What does the style of a house say about the people who live in it? What do the furniture and decorations inside of the house say? Give examples.

2. What are some different styles of houses around the world? What are some things that influence what houses look like, how people build them, and what materials they use in different areas of the world? Give examples.

LANGUAGE FOCUS

SIMPLE PRESENT NON-ACTION VERBS

Non-action Verbs			
believe	know	prefer	taste*
hate*	like*	remember*	think*
have*	love*	see	understand
hear	need	smell*	want

* These verbs can also be action verbs, but it's not common.

- We don't use some verbs in the present progressive. We call these **non-action** or stative **verbs**. They describe a state, not an action. We use the simple present with these verbs.

A. *Circle the correct form of the verb that completes each sentence.*

1. I (live / am living) in an old house right now.
2. I (love / am loving) old houses.
3. I (prefer / am preferring) an old house to a new house.
4. It (needs / is needing) new paint.
5. I (want / am wanting) to put a new bathroom in my house.
6. I (know / am knowing) it needs many things.
7. I (am decorating / decorate) the bedroom now.
8. My brother (helps / is helping) me at the moment.

B. *Work with a partner. Ask each other the following questions: What do you like about a house? What don't you like? What do you want in your dream house? Use complete sentences.*

PRONUNCIATION

INTONATION TO SHOW SURPRISE

A. *Listen to the conversations. Notice the rising and falling intonation. Then practice the dialogues with your partner.*

1. **A:** I live in a farmhouse. [↓]

   B: A farmhouse? [↑]

2. **A:** This house has ten rooms. [↓]

   B: Ten rooms? [↑]

B. *Listen to the conversations. Mark the rising and falling intonation next to each line. Then practice with your partner.*

1. **A:** That house is called a saltbox house. [ ]

   B: A saltbox house? [ ]

2. **A:** It's over one hundred years old. [ ]

   B: One hundred years old? [ ]

3. **A:** My friend lives in a shotgun house. [ ]

   B: A shotgun house? [ ]

4. **A:** The house only has two rooms. [ ]

   B: Only two rooms? [ ]

CONVERSATION

A. *Listen to the conversation. Then listen again and repeat.*

Ajay: Hey, Susan! <u>What's up?</u>

Susan: Well, I finally bought a farmhouse. It's <u>like a dream come true</u>!

Ajay: That's great! I know that's what you always wanted. Are you happy?

Susan: Yes! I'm so happy that I'm <u>at a loss for words</u>.

Do you know these expressions? What do you think they mean?

> What's up?   like a dream come true   at a loss for words

B. *Work with a partner. Practice a part of the conversation. Replace the underlined words with the words below.*

Ajay: Hey, Susan! What's up?

Susan: Well, I finally bought a farmhouse. It's <u>like a dream come true</u>!

> what I always wanted   everything I wished for

C. Your Turn. *Write a new conversation. Use some of the words below and your own ideas. Practice the conversation with a partner.*

> What's up?   like a dream come true   at a loss for words

Go to page 155 for the Internet Activity.

| DID YOU KNOW? | • In Indonesia, native people such as the Korowai and Kombai live in tree houses deep in the forest. Some of these houses are 130 feet (39.6 meters) high.
• The Masai people in Africa live in small houses that the women make from cow dung.
• Over 15,000 people live on houseboats in Great Britain. |  |

UNIT 14

WHAT IS SOME TRADITIONAL CLOTHING FROM AROUND THE WORLD?

you listen

before

Answer these questions.

1. What are some names of traditional clothing from around the world?

2. In what country or countries do women wear saris?

3. What traditional clothing do you think is beautiful?

VOCABULARY

MEANING

🎧 *Listen to the talk. Then write the correct words in the blanks.*

cloth	matches	plain	slip
loose	patterns	scarf	wrap

1. That blue sweater _____ the color of your eyes.
2. I have a silk _____ that I wear under my dress.
3. Peggy's going to make a blouse from soft cotton _____.
4. Frank's shirt is very _____ because it has one color and a simple design.
5. It's very cold. Put this _____ around you and you'll be warm.
6. My pants were too _____ around the waist, so I fixed them to make them smaller.
7. The sari was too big for the girl. She had to _____ it around herself several times.
8. The shirt had colorful flower _____ on it.

WORDS THAT GO TOGETHER

Write the correct words in the blanks.

social classes	tight fitting	vary from

1. This dress is too _____. I think I need a bigger size.
2. The wealthy, the poor, and those in the middle all belong to different _____.
3. The clothes that I wear in the winter _____ the clothes that I wear in the summer.

USE

Work with a partner to answer the questions. Use complete sentences.

1. When do people often wear *plain* clothes?
2. When do you wear a *scarf*?

(continued)

3. What do you like to *wrap* around you?

4. What color *matches* your eyes?

5. What are your favorite *patterns* on clothing?

6. What do you like to wear that's *tight fitting*?

7. What is your favorite kind of *cloth* for a shirt or blouse?

8. How do clothes *vary from* one season to another?

COMPREHENSION: LONG TALK

UNDERSTANDING THE LISTENING

Listen to the talk. Then circle the letter of the correct answer.

1. What do Indian women like about the sari?

   a. It's simple and stylish.
   b. It's expensive and modern.
   c. It's plain and useful.

2. What does the pattern and style of a sari tell us?

   a. the area it comes from
   b. how much it costs
   c. how old it is

3. What is the great advantage of a sari?

   a. It's not expensive.
   b. It's tight fitting.
   c. It looks nice on all women.

REMEMBERING DETAILS

Listen to the talk again. Then write the correct words in the blanks.

1. The sari style is _____ years old.

2. *Sati* means _____ in Sanskrit.

3. The material for a sari is about _____ long.

4. A woman wraps her sari around her _____.

5. A woman puts the pallu over her _____ shoulder.

6. The blouse a woman wears under her sari matches the color of her

   _____.

TAKING NOTES: Traditional Clothing

🎧 *Listen and write notes about the description. Which kind of traditional clothing does it describe?*

kimono

sarong

COMPREHENSION: SHORT CONVERSATIONS

🎧 *Listen to the conversations. Then circle the letter of the correct answer.*

CONVERSATION 1

1. What does the woman want to buy?

   a. a shirt   **b.** a dress   **c.** some cloth

CONVERSATION 2

2. Which shirt is the man going to wear?

   a. the one with stripes   **b.** the one with patterns   **c.** the plain one

CONVERSATION 3

3. Why is the man upset about spilling coffee on his shirt?

   a. It's a new shirt.   **b.** He doesn't have time to wash it.   **c.** It's the only one that matches his pants.

DISCUSSION

Discuss the answers to these questions with your classmates.

1. What is a traditional style of clothing in your country? What does it look like? What kind of cloth is it made from? Who wears it and when?
2. What style of clothing do you like to wear? Why? Which is more important to you, style or comfort?
3. What is your favorite style of clothing from another country? Why?

CRITICAL THINKING

Work with a partner. Ask each other the following questions. Discuss your answers.

1. What does it mean to be stylish? Why is it important to so many people? Do you think people put too much importance on style today? Why or why not?

2. What do clothes tell us about the person wearing them? What do your clothes say about you?

LANGUAGE FOCUS

INDIRECT OBJECT: *TO* AND *FOR*

- Some sentences have two objects after a verb: a direct object and an indirect object. A direct object answers the question *what* or *who*. An **indirect object** answers the question *to whom* or *what*.

Subject	Verb	Direct Object	Indirect Object
My mother	sent	a dress	**to** me.

- We can also put the indirect object before the direct object. Then we do not use the preposition *to*.

  My mother sent me a dress.

- We use *for* with the indirect object with some verbs. With these verbs, the direct object comes first. Then *for* + indirect object follows.

- With these verbs we use *for* + indirect object: *make, get, buy, answer, fix, open, prepare, pronounce.*

Subject	Verb	Direct Object	Indirect Object
My mother	made	a dress	**for** me.

  CORRECT: *The teacher pronounced the words for me.*
  NOT CORRECT: *The teacher pronounced me the words.*

- With the verbs *make, get,* and *buy* we can use *for* or not use *for*.

  My mother made a dress for me. OR My mother made me a dress.

A. *Complete the sentences with* to *or* for.

1. He gave the envelope _____ me.
2. She prepared the dress _____ her.
3. I gave my credit card _____ the salesperson.
4. She fixed the length of the dress _____ me.
5. She opened the box _____ me.
6. I explained my problem _____ her.

B. *Work with a partner. Imagine it's his or her birthday. Say four things you will do. Use* to *and* for *and the verbs below.*

give   send   write   get

EXAMPLE: I will get a birthday card for him.

PRONUNCIATION

REDUCED FORM OF *TO*

A. *We usually reduce the pronunciation of* to. *Listen to the sentences and notice the short and weak pronunciation of* to.

1. She gave it to me.
2. I showed the dress to him.
3. She handed the dress to me.
4. He introduced me to her.
5. I sent it to him.
6. I repeated it to her.

B. *Work with a partner. Practice saying the sentences above.*

CONVERSATION

A. *Listen to the conversation. Then listen again and repeat.*

Mia: I'm wearing my new coat. Look, it matches my scarf.
Rafi: Beautiful! <u>You wear it well.</u>
Mia: Thank you. <u>The nice thing about</u> it is that it keeps me warm, too.
Rafi: That's important. <u>After all</u>, it's cold outside!

Do you know these expressions? What do you think they mean?

> You wear it well.   The nice thing about   After all

B. *Work with a partner. Practice a part of the conversation. Replace the underlined words with the words below.*

Mia: I'm wearing my new coat. Look, it matches my scarf.
Rafi: Beautiful! <u>You wear it well.</u>

> It's very flattering.   It's lovely.

C. Your Turn. *Write a new conversation. Use some of the words below and your own ideas. Practice the conversation with a partner.*

> You wear it well.   The nice thing about   After all

 Go to page 155 for the Internet Activity.

DID YOU KNOW?	• The Mexican sombrero hat is supposed to make shade for the whole body. • American cowboys wore a hat called a ten-gallon hat, but it can't even hold one gallon of liquid. • In the Netherlands, the traditional shoes are wooden.

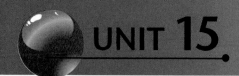

WHAT ARE SOME MAN-MADE ISLANDS?

before you listen

Answer these questions.

1. What are some man-made islands you know of?

2. Who lives on man-made islands?

3. What can man-made islands be made of?

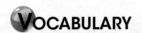
MEANING

Listen to the talk. Then write the correct words in the blanks.

celebrities	floats	ponds	stream
concrete	paradise	soil	waterfall

1. Many _____ own homes on man-made islands.

2. The water went over the mountain and made a beautiful _____.

3. The island _____ on the water in the ocean.

4. They're making a new _____ walkway on the island from cement, sand, and water.

5. We're so happy on this island that it feels like _____.

6. We're going to make _____ in our garden and put fish in them.

7. There are many different plants on the island because the _____ is very healthy.

8. The water in the _____ flowed over the land.

WORDS THAT GO TOGETHER

Write the correct words in the blanks.

in the shape of	off the coast of	well-known

1. The woman wanted to live on an island _____ Mexico.

2. A famous and _____ scientist is going to speak at our college today.

3. The artist built sculptures on the island _____ wild animals.

USE

Work with a partner to answer the questions. Use complete sentences.

1. Who are two of your favorite *celebrities*?

2. Where is a place that seems like *paradise*?

3. What is something that *floats* in the air?

4. Where is there a famous *waterfall*?

5. Where can you find a *stream*?

6. What is something made from *concrete*?

7. What kinds of life can you find in *ponds*?

8. Who is a *well-known* world leader?

COMPREHENSION: LONG TALK

UNDERSTANDING THE LISTENING

Listen to the talk. Then circle the letter of the correct answer.

1. What is special about the man-made islands off the coast of Dubai?

   a. They form different shapes.
   b. Anyone can go and live on them.
   c. They are close to Dubai.

2. How do people usually build man-made islands?

   a. from any material they can find
   b. from rocks and sand
   c. from tons of concrete

3. How did Rishi Sowa make his island?

   a. from soil and concrete
   b. from bottles
   c. from trees

REMEMBERING DETAILS

Listen to the talk again. Circle T if the sentence is true. Circle F if the sentence is false.

1. The Palm Islands are in the United Kingdom.   T   F

2. The islands that make up The World are in the shape of Europe.   T   F

3. Wealthy people have homes on The World.   T   F

4. Rishi Sowa is a wealthy celebrity.   T   F

5. A sandstorm destroyed Rishi Sowa's first island.   T   F

6. There's a stream and a waterfall on Rishi Sowa's island.   T   F

TAKING NOTES: Man-made Islands

🎧 *Listen and write notes about the description. Which island does it describe?*

The World

The Palm Islands

COMPREHENSION: SHORT CONVERSATIONS

🎧 *Listen to the conversations. Then circle the letter of the correct answer.*

CONVERSATION 1

1. What won't the man see on his trip to Hong Kong?

   a. the Boat City
   b. Hong Kong Disneyland
   c. the Stanley Market

CONVERSATION 2

2. Why did the man miss the boat to No Man's Island?

   a. His watch was wrong.
   b. The boat left at 8 o'clock.
   c. The boat left late.

CONVERSATION 3

3. Who is the woman speaking to?

   a. a travel agent
   b. a friend
   c. a salesman in a shop

DISCUSSION

Discuss the answers to these questions with your classmates.

1. What are some reasons why people make man-made islands? What is the difference between islands like The Palm Islands and Rishi Sowa's Spiral Islands?
2. Do you think life on a man-made island is different from life on a natural island? Why or why not?
3. Are there any islands in the world where you want to live? Why or why not?

CRITICAL THINKING

Work with a partner. Ask each other the following questions. Discuss your answers.

1. The Palm Islands and The World are for wealthy people only. What are other places in the world where wealthy people live? Do you think it is right to have places where only the wealthy can live? Why or why not?

2. Imagine you are building your own man-made island. What are you making it from? What does it look like? What is on the island? Who is on the island with you?

LANGUAGE FOCUS

INDEFINITE PRONOUNS

	Some-	**Any-**	**No-**
People	someone somebody	anyone anybody	no one nobody
Things	something	anything	nothing

- We use *some-* (*something, someone, somebody*), and *no-* (*nothing, no one, nobody*) in positive statements.

    I see someone on the island.
    There's nobody on the island.

- We use *any-* (*anything, anyone, anybody*) in negative statements.

    I don't see anyone.

- We can use *some-* or *any-* in questions.

    Do you need something? OR Do you need anything?

A. *Circle the correct indefinite pronoun.*

1. I can hear (something / anything).
2. I think there's (someone / anyone) at the door.
3. I'm sure there's (nobody / anybody) there.
4. There isn't (anyone / someone) there.
5. You have (something / anything) wrong with your ears!
6. I don't have (something / anything) wrong with my ears.

B. *Work with a partner. Think of something or somebody. Ask each other questions to find out what or who your partner is thinking about. Use indefinite pronouns.*

EXAMPLE:

A: This is something you find in an office.

B: Is it something you use every day?

PRONUNCIATION

WORD STRESS FOR CLARIFICATION

Sometimes one word in a sentence is stressed more than the others. This is to clarify the meaning of the sentence.

EXAMPLE: The island is made of <u>bottles</u>. (not earth)

A. *Listen to the sentences. Underline the words that are stressed.*

1. They made three hundred islands. (not four)
2. The islands have shapes. (not just any shape)
3. She is going to Hawaii. (not Sicily)
4. Rishi Sowa is an artist. (not a businessperson)
5. He owns the island. (He doesn't just rent it.)
6. It's his second island. (not his first)

B. *Work with a partner. Take turns reading the sentences above. Make sure you stress the underlined words for clarification.*

CONVERSATION

A. *Listen to the conversation. Then listen again and repeat.*

Ani: I'm not going to Baker Island on vacation this year. I'm going to Echo Lake instead.

Su: I'm happy to know you're going somewhere else <u>for a change</u>! What's Echo Lake? I don't know anything about it.

Ani: Well, it's deep in a forest and it has a man-made island in the middle of it.

Su: Really? <u>That's crazy!</u> <u>It sounds like</u> a very interesting place.

Do you know these expressions? What do you think they mean?

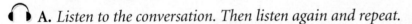

for a change   That's crazy!   It sounds like

B. *Work with a partner. Practice a part of the conversation. Replace the underlined words with the words below.*

Ani: I'm not going to Baker Island on vacation this year. I'm going to Echo Lake instead.

Su: I'm happy to know you're going somewhere else <u>for a change</u>! What's Echo Lake? I don't know anything about it.

finally   after all these years

C. Your Turn. *Write a new conversation. Use some of the words below and your own ideas. Practice the conversation with a partner.*

for a change   That's crazy!   It sounds like

Go to page 156 for the Internet Activity.

| DID YOU KNOW? | • People built an island called Thilafushi in the middle of the Maldive Islands to dump garbage. It now has thousands of tons of garbage.
• Fadiouth in Senegal, Africa, is a man-made island made up of mostly clam shells. It has a population of more than 40,000 people.
• Kansai Internationl Airport is on a man-made island off the coast of Japan. It's so big that you can see it from space! |  |

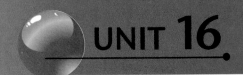
WHAT DO YOU KNOW ABOUT SPORTS?

before you listen

Answer these questions.

1. What kinds of sports do you play with a bat and a ball?

2. What is the most popular sport in your country?

3. What is your favorite sport?

VOCABULARY

MEANING

Listen to the talk. Then write the correct words in the blanks.

bat	field	last	teams
coach	flat	once	umpires

1. This ball lost all its air and now it's as _____ as a board.

2. We have a great _____ for our team. He makes us work really hard, so we usually win.

3. The children are using a piece of wood as a _____ to hit the ball.

4. Our team plays on an open area of land, or _____.

5. The _____ make sure that the teams play by the rules of the game.

6. Our game didn't _____ very long because it started to pour rain.

7. The groups of people who play sports are on different _____.

8. Soccer was _____ a popular sport at our school, but not anymore.

WORDS THAT GO TOGETHER

Write the correct words in the blanks.

similar to	take a break	the number one

1. This hat is _____ yours. Only the color is different.

2. _____ sport in my country is soccer. Many people play it.

3. When I work hard, I like to _____ so I can rest a little.

USE

Work with a partner to answer the questions. Use complete sentences.

1. What are some sports people play on a *field*?

2. For what sports do you need a *bat*?

3. Why is it important to have a *coach*?

4. What is something that is *flat*?

(continued)

5. At what times of day do people often *take a break*?

6. What is *the number one* sports team in your opinion?

7. Why do teams need *umpires*?

8. How long does your favorite sports game usually *last*?

COMPREHENSION: LONG TALK

UNDERSTANDING THE LISTENING

Listen to the talk. Then circle the letter of the correct answer.

1. In what countries is cricket most popular?

   a. anyplace where baseball is popular

   b. those once under British control

   c. England and the United States

2. How is cricket similar to baseball?

   a. It has the same number of players.

   b. It also has bats and balls.

   c. It lasts for the same amount of time.

3. How are cricket and baseball different?

   a. One uses a bat and the other doesn't.

   b. The number of teams that play is different.

   c. The fields are different shapes and sizes.

REMEMBERING DETAILS

Listen to the talk again. Then write the correct words in the blanks.

1. _____ is a more popular sport than cricket.

2. Cricket is the number one sport in _____.

3. Cricket started in _____.

4. A cricket team has eleven players, but a baseball team has _____.

5. Both cricket and baseball use a ball and a _____.

6. A baseball field is shaped like a _____.

TAKING NOTES: Sports

🎧 *Listen and write notes about the description. Which sport does it describe?*

soccer

rugby

COMPREHENSION: SHORT CONVERSATIONS

🎧 *Listen to the conversations. Then circle the letter of the correct answer.*

CONVERSATION 1

1. Why is the man unhappy with the restaurant?

   a. His food is cold.

   b. His food doesn't taste good.

   c. He doesn't like the way it looks.

CONVERSATION 2

2. Why is the woman upset?

   a. It's raining.

   b. The field is wet.

   c. The game is lasting too long.

CONVERSATION 3

3. Where is the man?

   a. at work

   b. on a sports field

   c. at a sports shop

DISCUSSION

Discuss the answers to these questions with your classmates.

1. Do you like to play sports? Why or why not? Do you like to watch sports? Why or why not? Which sports do you think are the most exciting? Which sports do you think are the least exciting? Why?

(continued)

2. What is a "top athlete"? How do people become top athletes? What qualities and characteristics do you need to become a top athlete?

3. The same sports aren't popular in all countries. Name some sports that are played in different places around the world, such as Alaska, Hawaii, the Netherlands, and Egypt. How do the society, government, and location of a country affect the sports that are played there?

CRITICAL THINKING

Work with a partner. Ask each other the following questions. Discuss your answers.

1. In most countries, sports are very important to the people and even the government. Why are sports so important? What do sports do for governments, society in general, and individuals? What are the benefits of sports? Can sports ever cause problems? Why or why not?

2. Do you think sports are good for children? Why or why not? What are the advantages and disadvantages of playing sports as a child? Do you think that today's parents push their children too much when they play sports? Why or why not?

LANGUAGE FOCUS

AS . . . AS / NOT AS . . . AS / LESS . . . THAN

(not) as + adjective + *as*	*less* + adjective + *than*
Cricket is *(not) as fun as* soccer.	Cricket is *less popular than* soccer.

- We use *as* + **adjective** + *as* to say that two things or people are the same in some way.
- We use *not as* + **adjective** + *as* to say that two things or people are different in some way.
- We use *less* + **adjective** + *than* with a long adjective (two syllables or more) except for most adjectives ending in -*y*. We don't use *less* + adjective + *than* with one-syllable adjectives.

A. *Rewrite the sentences to have the same meaning. Use* less . . . than *where possible. If it isn't possible, write* No change.

1. Some people think cricket isn't as exciting as soccer.

   <u>*Some people think cricket is less exciting than soccer.*</u>

2. Soccer isn't as rough as rugby.

   _____

3. This game isn't as good as the last game.

   _____

4. This team isn't as talented as the other team.

   _____

5. This game isn't as enjoyable as the last game.

   _____

6. That player isn't as fast as the others.

   _____

B. *Work with a partner. Compare your physical characteristics. Use* as + adjective + as *and* not as + adjective + as.

PRONUNCIATION

THAN AND AS

A. *Listen and underline the stressed words.*

EXAMPLE: <u>This</u> <u>game</u> isn't as <u>good</u> as the <u>last one</u>.

1. Hockey is less popular than soccer.
2. Cricket isn't as exciting as ice hockey.
3. This game is less enjoyable than the previous one.
4. This game isn't as fun as the other one.
5. The new player is as old as I am.

B. *Listen again and repeat.*

 CONVERSATION

🎧 **A.** *Listen to the conversation. Then listen again and repeat.*

Ren: Do you know what time our tennis practice is? <u>I don't have a clue.</u>

Mark: It's at three o'clock, of course. <u>By the way</u>, do you like our new coach?

Ren: Yes, he's great! <u>In fact</u>, I think he's much better than our last coach.

Mark: I do, too. We're going to be much better players because of him.

Do you know these expressions? What do you think they mean?

I don't have a clue.	By the way	In fact

B. *Work with a partner. Practice a part of the conversation. Replace the underlined words with the words below.*

Ren: Do you know what time our tennis practice is? <u>I don't have a clue.</u>

Mark: It's at three o'clock, of course. By the way, do you like our new coach?

I have no idea.	I don't remember.

C. Your Turn. *Write a new conversation. Use some of the words below and your own ideas. Practice the conversation with a partner.*

I don't have a clue.	By the way	In fact

🖱️ *Go to page 156 for the Internet Activity.*

DID YOU KNOW?
- Andy Roddick, a tennis player from the United States, hit the fastest recorded tennis serve—155 miles (249.5 kilometers) per hour!
- Over 700 million people around the world watched the final World Cup soccer game between Spain and The Netherlands in 2010.
- Russia banned table tennis/ping pong early in the twentieth century because they believed it was harmful to players' eyesight.

WHAT DO YOU KNOW ABOUT AUSTRALIA?

you listen

before

Answer these questions.

1. Where is Australia?

2. What are some places to see in Australia?

3. What are some unusual animals that live in Australia?

VOCABULARY

MEANING

Listen to the talk. Then write the correct words in the blanks.

continent	forever	isolated	resorts
definitely	hemisphere	perfect	warn

1. I _____ can't go to Australia with you. I have to work.

2. I'm having so much fun on my vacation that I want it to last _____ and never end.

3. The _____ along this beach are beautiful places to stay and enjoy a vacation.

4. This area is so clean and unspoiled that it's _____.

5. This hotel is too _____ from the others on the island. It's too far away.

6. This part of the beach is very dangerous. I will _____ the others in our tour group.

7. Australia is the smallest _____ of the seven on Earth.

8. Australia is in the southern half of Earth. It's in the Southern _____.

WORDS THAT GO TOGETHER

Write the correct words in the blanks.

low tide	natural wonders	sea life

1. In certain areas of the ocean such as coral reefs, there is a great variety of

   _____.

2. At _____, the sea pulls back from the shore.

3. There are places in nature that are so beautiful that we call them

   _____.

USE

Work with a partner to answer the questions. Use complete sentences.

1. What *continent* do you live on?
2. What *hemisphere* do you live in?
3. What is a place that has many *resorts*?
4. Why do people go to see the *natural wonders* of the world?
5. What do we see in the sand at *low tide*?
6. What do you think is *perfect*?
7. What is your favorite kind of *sea life*?
8. What do you *definitely* know about tomorrow?

COMPREHENSION: LONG TALK

UNDERSTANDING THE LISTENING

Listen to the talk. Then circle the letter of the correct answer.

1. What makes Australia unique?

   a. its size and wildlife   **b.** its cities and people   **c.** its location and resorts

2. What will the woman see at the Great Barrier Reef?

   a. bridges and buildings   **b.** empty, isolated places   **c.** beaches and resorts

3. Why does the man think the woman will not like the outback?

   a. because of the weather and the wildlife   **b.** because there are too many people there   **c.** because there isn't much to see

REMEMBERING DETAILS

Listen to the talk again. Circle T if the sentence is true. Circle F if the sentence is false.

1. Australia is the largest continent in the world.	T	F
2. There are more kangaroos than humans in Australia.	T	F
3. The Sydney Opera House is near the Great Barrier Reef.	T	F

(continued)

4. If it's summer in the Northern Hemisphere, it's winter in Australia.

        T   F

5. The Great Barrier Reef is in Queensland.

        T   F

6. Even in the summer, it's cold in the outback.

        T   F

TAKING NOTES: Coastal Areas of Australia

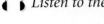 *Listen and write notes about the description. Which coastal area of Australia does it describe?*

(view from) the Great Ocean Road

the Great Barrier Reef

COMPREHENSION: SHORT CONVERSATIONS

Listen to the conversations. Then circle the letter of the correct answers.

CONVERSATION 1

1. What does the man want to do?

   a. take a break   **b.** go to the beach   **c.** tour the city

CONVERSATION 2

2. Why is the woman upset?

   a. She didn't like the desert.   **b.** She went to the mountains instead of the desert.   **c.** The man didn't tell her about the desert.

CONVERSATION 3

3. Where is the man?

   a. at a bookstore   **b.** at a travel agency   **c.** at a library

DISCUSSION

Discuss the answers to these questions with your classmates.

1. What is unique about your country? What special animals live there? What beautiful places are there to see?

2. What are some unique places to visit around the world? What makes them unique?

3. Do you want to visit Australia? Why or why not? What interests you the most about Australia? What interests you the least?

CRITICAL THINKING

Work with a partner. Ask each other the following questions. Discuss your answers.

1. Which do you prefer, a beautiful resort by the beach or a trip to the outback where you are closer to nature and have less comforts? Why? What kinds of people like to visit places like the outback? Why do people want to go to isolated places that are difficult to travel to?

2. When you travel, what do you like to see most? For example, do you like cities or places in nature? What are the benefits of travel?

LANGUAGE FOCUS

IF . . . (PRESENT), WILL . . .

If Clause (Present)	Main Clause *(will/won't)*
If you **go** to the beach,	you**'ll miss** the tour.
Main Clause *(will/won't)*	*If* Clause (Present)
You**'ll miss** the tour	if you **go** to the beach.

- We use the future conditional to say that one situation in the future depends on another situation.
- A conditional sentence has a **main clause** and a dependent clause with *if* or an *if* **clause**.
- We use the simple present in the *if* clause and the future in the main clause.
- An *if* clause can come before or after a main clause. The meaning is the same. When the *if* clause comes first, we put a comma (,) after it.

A. *Complete the sentences with the correct form of the verbs. Use contractions.*

1. If you (go) _____ to Sydney, you'll see the famous Sydney Opera House.
2. You (see) _____ the Great Barrier Reef if you travel to Queensland.
3. If you (swim) _____ around the Great Barrier Reef, you'll see tropical fish.
4. You'll see kangaroos if you (travel) _____ around Australia.
5. If you go to the outback it (be) _____ hot.
6. You (not / like) _____ the outback if you go.

B. *Work with a partner. A friend from another country is coming to visit you for the first time next week. They want to see your city. Make a plan of places to take them. Provide options in case they don't like your plan.*

EXAMPLE: I'll take them to my favorite fish restaurant. If they don't like fish, I'll take them to a vegetarian restaurant.

PRONUNCIATION

THE SOUND /l/ IN CONTRACTIONS

A. *The sound /l/ is difficult to hear. Listen to the sentences. Then circle the letter of the sentence you hear.*

1. **a.** You like it.
   b. You'll like it.
2. **a.** I go there.
   b. I'll go there.
3. **a.** We travel there.
   b. We'll travel there.
4. **a.** We go there.
   b. We'll go there.
5. **a.** They see him.
   b. They'll see him.
6. **a.** We swim there.
   b. We'll swim there.

B. *Work with a partner. Practice saying the sentences above.*

CONVERSATION

A. *Listen to the conversation. Then listen again and repeat.*

Valentina: I want to go to Australia, but I also really want to go to New Zealand.

April: Oh, New Zealand is <u>a different story</u>! You must go there, too. It's beautiful!

Valentina: Well, everyone knows that *you* like it. You <u>can't miss</u> those huge pictures in your office!

April: Well, <u>let me tell you</u>, you'll love it there, too. I know you.

Do you know these expressions? What do you think they mean?

a different story   can't miss   let me tell you

B. *Work with a partner. Practice a part of the conversation. Replace the underlined words with the words below.*

Valentina: I want to go to Australia, but I also really want to go to New Zealand.

April: Oh, New Zealand is <u>a different story</u>! You must go there, too. It's beautiful!

something else   totally different

C. Your Turn. *Write a new conversation. Use some of the words below and your own ideas. Practice the conversation with a partner.*

a different story   can't miss   let me tell you

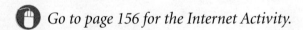

Go to page 156 for the Internet Activity.

DID YOU KNOW?	• Koala bears, native animals of Australia, have fingerprints that are almost the same as humans' fingerprints. • The Great Barrier Reef is the world's biggest structure made by living things. • The architect for the Sydney Opera House was a Danish man named Jorn Utzon.	

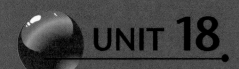

WHAT ARE SOME NATIONAL EMBLEMS?

before you listen

Answer these questions.

1. What animal has great meaning in your country?

2. Why is that animal so important?

3. What does it mean when an animal is a symbol of something? Give an example.

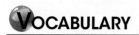

MEANING

Listen to the talk. Then write the correct words in the blanks.

admire	coins	independence	pleasant
amazing	courage	legend	remarkable

1. The new design for our country's flag is _____. It's beautiful!

2. The men showed _____ when they faced many dangers to save people from the storm.

3. African nations fought to get their _____ from Europeans who had control over them.

4. Our people have a _____, or old story, about a bear.

5. She is a very nice and _____ person.

6. These flat pieces of metal are _____ that the people use as money.

7. The woman received an award for the _____ work she did to help people during the war.

8. I _____ and greatly respect my grandparents for their wisdom and knowledge about their country's history.

WORDS THAT GO TOGETHER

Write the correct words in the blanks.

a broken heart	long life	national emblem

1. The picture on the coin is a symbol of health and _____.

2. The boy had _____ after he lost his bird. He was very sad and cried often.

3. The maple leaf is on the Canadian flag because it's the country's _____.

USE

Work with a partner to answer the questions. Use complete sentences.

1. What is a way in which a person shows *courage*?
2. Who do you *admire*?
3. When did you have *a broken heart*?
4. What did you see recently that was *amazing*?
5. What pictures are on the *coins* of your country?
6. What is a *national emblem* of your country?
7. How do you show your *independence*?
8. What do you do in order to live a *long life*?

COMPREHENSION: LONG TALK

UNDERSTANDING THE LISTENING

🎧 *Listen to the talk. Then circle the letter of the correct answer.*

1. What does the bald eagle symbolize to Americans?

   a. war and power   **b.** peace   **c.** freedom

2. What does a Guatemalan legend say will happen to a quetzal when it's captured?

   a. It flies away.   **b.** It dies.   **c.** It gets stronger.

3. How do countries choose their animal symbols?

   a. The animals have qualities they admire.   **b.** There are many of those animals living in their country.   **c.** The animals help the people in some way.

REMEMBERING DETAILS

🎧 *Listen to the talk again. Then answer these questions.*

1. What does the legend say about the bald eagle?
2. In Japan, what is the crane a symbol of?
3. How many paper cranes do you need to make to have good health?
4. What is the quetzal a symbol of in Guatemala?
5. In which country is the lion a symbol of strength, courage, and pride?
6. What do people admire the elephant for in Thailand?

TAKING NOTES: Birds

🎧 *Listen and write notes about the description. Which bird does it describe?*

bald eagle

crane

COMPREHENSION: SHORT CONVERSATIONS

🎧 *Listen to the conversations. Then circle the letter of the correct answer.*

CONVERSATION 1

1. What will the man probably do today?

   a. go to the zoo
   b. work at the bird shelter
   c. work on his paper

CONVERSATION 2

2. Who is the man talking to?

   a. a painter
   b. a student
   c. a teacher

CONVERSATION 3

3. What does the woman have to do?

   a. pack her suitcases
   b. make hotel reservations
   c. buy her plane tickets

DISCUSSION

Discuss the answers to these questions with your classmates.

1. What characteristics do people usually give to the following animals: ox, donkey, beaver, rooster, camel, wolf, lamb?

2. What animal do you admire the most? Why? What animal do you dislike the most? Why?

(continued)

3. Do you think people look and act like some animals? Why or why not? What animal do you think you have characteristics of? Why?

CRITICAL THINKING

Work with a partner. Ask each other the following questions. Discuss your answers.

1. Even the earliest civilizations used animals as symbols. Why do you think this is so? Why are symbols so important to people and countries?
2. What are some animals that appear in folk stories and fairy tales? Do you think these animals are symbols in these stories? Why or why not?

LANGUAGE FOCUS

HAVE TO AND MUST

Have to/Don't have to		
I/We/You/They	**have to/don't have to**	go there.
He/She/It	**has to/doesn't have to**	go there.

Must/Must not		
I/You/He/She/It/We/They	**must/must not**	go there.

- We use **have to** for something that is necessary or an obligation. *Have to* is not as strong as *must*. *Have to* is the same as *need to*.
- We use **don't have to/doesn't have to** for something that is not necessary. There is a choice.
- We use **must** to say something is necessary or very important. We use *must* for laws, rules, or strong advice.
- We use **must not** when something is against the rules. It is forbidden to do it.

A. *Complete the sentences with the positive or negative form of* have to *or* must.

1. A country _____ have a flag. It's necessary.
2. The national emblem of a country _____ be a bird. It can be an animal, too.

3. The animal or bird for the emblem _____ have good or strong qualities.

4. The emblem _____ be on the flag. It's not necessary.

5. In many countries, it's against the law to destroy the flag. You _____ destroy the flag.

6. The emblem _____ be a real animal. It can be an imaginary animal like a dragon.

B. *Work with a partner. What are six things you have to or don't have to do in your English class?*

EXAMPLE: We have to take tests.

PRONUNCIATION

MUST

A. *Listen to the sentences. Notice how the word* must *is weak in some sentences and stressed in others. Underline* must *once when it is not stressed. Underline it twice when it is stressed.*

1. You must do your homework.
2. I must call John later.
3. It's getting late and I must go soon.
4. You must go to the zoo. The baby tiger is so cute!
5. I must start losing some weight.
6. You must take your dog to the vet right away. He looks very sick.

B. *Listen to the sentences again and repeat.*

CONVERSATION

A. *Listen to the conversation. Then listen again and repeat.*

   Alec: What's that dance you're doing?
   Elena: It's the Bear Dance. The bear is very important to the Native Americans. It's a symbol of power. By the way, my family is Native American.
   Alec: It's no wonder you dance it so well! It looks like second nature to you.
   Elena: Thank you! Come to think of it, I have a video of me and my family dancing the Bear Dance together. Look at this!

Do you know these expressions? What do you think they mean?

> It's no wonder   like second nature   Come to think of it

B. *Work with a partner. Practice a part of the conversation. Replace the underlined words with the words below.*

    Alec: It's no wonder you dance it so well! It looks <u>like second nature to you</u>.

  Elena: Thank you! Come to think of it, I have a video of me and my family dancing the Bear Dance together. Look at this!

> effortless   very natural

C. Your Turn. *Write a new conversation. Use some of the words below and your own ideas. Practice the conversation with a partner.*

> It's no wonder   like second nature   Come to think of it

 Go to page 157 for the Internet Activity.

DID YOU KNOW?	• A full-grown bald eagle can kill a young deer and fly away with it. • The most common color found on national flags is red. • Nepal's flag is the only national flag in the world that has more than four sides.	

WHAT DO YOU KNOW ABOUT THE ANCIENT GREEKS?

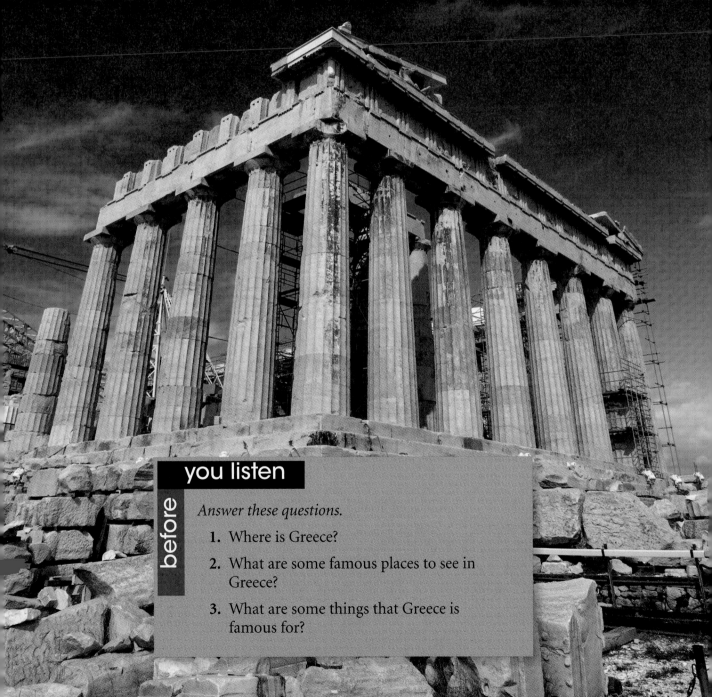

you listen

before

Answer these questions.

1. Where is Greece?
2. What are some famous places to see in Greece?
3. What are some things that Greece is famous for?

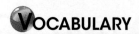

MEANING

Listen to the talk. Then write the correct words in the blanks.

citizen	goal	soldiers	temple
columns	military	state	vote

1. Those men with uniforms are _____ who are fighting for their country.

2. Anita's _____ is to go to Greece, so she's working hard to save money.

3. The building has many beautiful _____ that hold it up.

4. Our country has a strong _____ to take care of matters of war.

5. If you're a _____, you have a right to live in a certain country.

6. Tomorrow our class will _____ to decide if we'll go to Greece or to Italy this summer.

7. Our _____ forms a part of our country, but it has its own local government.

8. That beautiful _____ is a place where people worship and have religious ceremonies.

WORDS THAT GO TOGETHER

Write the correct words in the blanks.

get rid of	made laws	took place

1. In ancient Greece, only men _____ that the people had to follow.

2. I don't want these old teacups from Greece. I want to _____ them.

3. The meetings _____ early in the morning in the center of the city.

USE

Work with a partner to answer the questions. Use complete sentences.

1. What is a *goal* of yours?
2. When do people *vote* in your country?
3. What is a job of the *military* in your country?
4. Of what country are you a *citizen*?
5. What do *soldiers* usually wear?
6. When do you want to *get rid of* something?
7. What kind of buildings often have *columns*?
8. What important event *took place* recently in your life?

COMPREHENSION: LONG TALK

UNDERSTANDING THE LISTENING

Listen to the talk. Then circle the letter of the correct answer.

1. What was Sparta known for?
   a. its democratic government
   b. its military
   c. its healthy citizens

2. Why did the Greeks build the Parthenon?
   a. for Athena
   b. for the government
   c. for sports training

3. Who ruled the country in ancient Greece?
   a. a few men
   b. male citizens
   c. one man

REMEMBERING DETAILS

Listen to the talk again. Then write the correct words in the blanks.

1. The ancient Greeks held the Olympic Games once every _____ years.
2. They trained Spartan boys to be _____.
3. The Greeks built the Parthenon in _____.
4. The Greeks built _____ to worship their gods and goddesses.
5. The Greeks started a form of government called _____.
6. All male citizens over _____ years old could vote.

TAKING NOTES: Places in Ancient Greece

🎧 *Listen and write notes about the description. Which place in ancient Greece does it describe?*

Acropolis, Athens, Greece

Olympia, Elis, Greece

COMPREHENSION: SHORT CONVERSATIONS

🎧 *Listen to the conversations. Then circle the letter of the correct answer.*

CONVERSATION 1

1. Where did the woman spend most of her time in Greece?

   a. Crete   **b.** Delphi   **c.** Athens

CONVERSATION 2

2. When did the man vote?

   a. in the morning   **b.** at noon   **c.** in the afternoon

CONVERSATION 3

3. Why did the man go to the Olympic Games?

   a. He was on a team.   **b.** His friend ran.   **c.** He had tickets.

DISCUSSION

Discuss the answers to these questions with your classmates.

1. What did the ancient Greeks give to civilizations that came later? What contributions to the world did your country make?
2. What is an old type of architecture in your country? Describe it. Does your country have modern buildings? What are some characteristics of modern architecture?
3. Are there religious buildings in your country? What do they look like?

CRITICAL THINKING

Work with a partner. Ask each other the following questions. Discuss your answers.

1. What rights do people have in a democracy? What are the advantages and disadvantages of democratic government? What other forms of government are there in the world today?

2. Do you like to study ancient history? Why or why not? Why is it important for people to study ancient civilizations? What can we learn from them?

LANGUAGE FOCUS

PAST *WH-* AND *YES/NO* QUESTIONS

WH- QUESTIONS			
Wh- Word	**Did**	**Subject**	**Base Verb**
What When Where Who How Why	did	I/you/he/she/we/they	see? go? stay? meet? travel? leave?

YES/NO QUESTIONS	
Question	**Answer**
Did I/you/he/she/we/they go?	No, I/you/he/she/we/they didn't. Yes, I/you/he/she/we/they did.

A. *Write Wh- questions for the answers. The underlined words will help you choose the correct question word.*

1. They trained the best soldiers in <u>Sparta</u>.

   <u>*Where did they train the best soldiers?*</u>

2. The Olympic Games took place <u>every four years</u>.

   _____

(continued)

3. The Parthenon was a famous temple in Athens.

_____

4. The kind of government they had was a democracy.

_____

5. People voted in Greece 2,500 years ago.

_____

6. The men voted.

_____

B. _Work with a partner. Take turns asking your partner questions about when he or she was a child._

EXAMPLE:

A: Where did you go to school?

B: I went to school near my house.

A: Did you take the bus to school?

B: Yes, I did.

 PRONUNCIATION

STRESS WITH AUXILIARY VERBS _DO/DID_

In questions that begin with _wh-_ question words (_what, when, where, who, why_), the auxiliary verbs **_do/did_** and the subject are not stressed when we speak fast.

A. _Listen and complete the sentence with the auxiliary verb and the subject._

1. What _____ do?
2. What _____ see?
3. When _____ end?
4. Where _____ go?
5. How _____ know?
6. Why _____ ask?

B. _Listen to the questions again and repeat._

CONVERSATION

A. *Listen to the conversation. Then listen again and repeat.*

Yoko: <u>I got into</u> that ancient history class I wanted.

Matt: Hey, that's great! I know you're really into history.

Yoko: I am! You're going to try out for the drama club, right?

Matt: <u>Without a doubt!</u> You know I love acting. Hey, I'll <u>let you know</u> if I get a part in *Julius Caesar*!

Do you know these expressions? What do you think they mean?

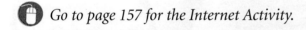

> I got into   Without a doubt!   let you know

B. *Work with a partner. Practice a part of the conversation. Replace the underlined words with the words below.*

Yoko: I am! You're going to try out for the drama club, right?

Matt: <u>Without a doubt!</u> You know I love acting. Hey, I'll let you know if I get a part in *Julius Caesar*!

> Definitely!   You bet!

C. Your Turn. *Write a new conversation. Use some of the words below and your own ideas. Practice the conversation with a partner.*

> I got into   Without a doubt!   let you know

Go to page 157 for the Internet Activity.

Go to page 157 for the Internet Activity.

DID YOU KNOW?	• The ancient Greeks thought wearing white to bed gave them pleasant dreams. • The ancient Greeks established the first library. • In ancient Greece, married women were not allowed to attend the Olympic Games. Women who did were thrown off a cliff.	

HOW DID THE NOBEL PEACE PRIZE START?

before you listen

Answer these questions.

1. Who is someone that received a Nobel Peace Prize?

2. What kinds of people do you think receive the Nobel Peace Prize?

3. Who do you think deserves to win the next Nobel Peace Prize?

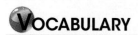

MEANING

Listen to the talk. Then write the correct words in the blanks.

chemist	dynamite	equivalent	support
destruction	economics	selects	will

1. A group of five people _____ who will receive the prize.

2. The winner of the prize had a lot of _____ from the people of her country.

3. In her _____, the woman wrote that she wanted to give all of her money to sick children after she died.

4. I enjoy my studies in _____ because I'm interested in business and money matters.

5. Engineers use _____ to blow up huge rocks and clear the way to build roads.

6. Marie Curie was a famous _____—she was a scientist who worked with chemicals.

7. The storm caused a lot of _____ and people from all over the world traveled to help clean up the mess.

8. There is no prize that is _____ to the Nobel Peace Prize. It's unique.

WORDS THAT GO TOGETHER

Write the correct words in the blanks.

consists of	gave instructions	prize winner

1. The _____ lifted the medal above his head so that the people could see it.

2. The group of writers _____ men and women from many countries around the world.

3. The woman _____ to the workers so that they knew exactly how to arrange the tables and chairs for the event.

USE

Work with a partner to answer the questions. Use complete sentences.

1. Why is it important to write a *will*?
2. What does your favorite meal *consist of*?
3. Where does a *chemist* usually work?
4. Why do businesses need people who study *economics*?
5. When is the last time you *gave instructions*?
6. Who do you know that is a *prize winner*?
7. What natural force sometimes causes great *destruction*?
8. What is a use for *dynamite*?

COMPREHENSION: LONG TALK

UNDERSTANDING THE LISTENING

🎧 *Listen to the talk. Then circle the letter of the correct answer.*

1. Why did Alfred Nobel create the Nobel Peace Prize?

    a. He wanted people to remember him as a man of peace.

    b. He worked all his life for world peace.

    c. He wanted people to work harder for world peace.

2. What instructions did Nobel leave in his will?

    a. who selects the winner and where they give the prize

    b. who the winners are and what countries they come from

    c. what people should remember about him

3. What are people not always happy about the Nobel Peace Prize committee?

    a. the number and kind of prizes they give

    b. the people they choose for the prizes

    c. the reasons why they give the prizes

REMEMBERING DETAILS

🎧 *Listen to the talk again. Circle* **T** *if the sentence is true. Circle* **F** *if the sentence is false.*

1. There are Nobel Peace Prizes for sports.   T   F

2. Alfred Nobel worked in medicine.   T   F

3. Alfred Nobel wanted people who help others to   T   F
   receive the Nobel Peace Prize.

4. They give the Nobel Peace Prize in Norway.   T   F

5. The Nobel Peace Prize committee selects a winner   T   F
   every four years.

6. The winner of the Nobel Peace Prize receives a medal.   T   F

TAKING NOTES: Nobel Peace Prize Winners

🎧 *Listen and write notes about the description. Which Nobel Peace Prize winner does it describe?*

Nelson Mandela

Dr. Martin Luther King Jr.

COMPREHENSION: SHORT CONVERSATIONS

🎧 *Listen to the conversations. Then circle the letter of the correct answer.*

CONVERSATION 1

1. Why is the man upset?

   a. His students are   **b.** He has no prizes   **c.** He doesn't know which
   unhappy.   for his students.   students to select for
                                                                     the prizes.

(continued)

CONVERSATION 2

2. What did the woman do in Sweden?

   a. She met with a famous chemist.

   b. She took an economics class.

   c. She went to the Nobel Museum.

CONVERSATION 3

3. Where is the woman working now?

   a. UNICEF

   b. the Red Cross

   c. Save the Children

DISCUSSION

Discuss the answers to these questions with your classmates.

1. What are some areas in which people get prizes for what they do? Did you ever receive a prize for something? If so, what was it for? How did it make you feel?

2. What work does the Red Cross do? What are some other organizations that help people?

3. What are some ways in which we can help others in our everyday lives? Why is it important to help other people?

CRITICAL THINKING

Work with a partner. Ask each other the following questions. Discuss your answers.

1. Why is it important to give prizes and reward people for the things they do? What is something you would really like to do to help people? What kind of prize would you like for it? Why?

2. Some world leaders received the Nobel Peace Prize after they started wars. Yet other people who worked their whole lives for peace never received a Nobel Peace Prize. Why do you think this happened? Do you think the Nobel Peace Prize should continue? Do you think the committee always does what Nobel wanted? Who do you think deserved a Nobel Peace Prize in the past?

PRESENT PERFECT

Statements	Questions and Answers
I/You/We/They**'ve (have)** worked there. I/You/We/They **haven't (have not)** worked there.	**Q: Have** I/you/we/they worked there? **A:** Yes, I/you/we/they **have**. No, I/you/we/they **haven't (have not)**.
He/She/It**'s (has)** worked there. He/She/It **hasn't (has not)** worked there.	**Q: Has** he/she/it worked there? **A:** Yes, he/she/it **has**. No, he/she/it **hasn't (has not)**.

- We form the **present perfect** with *have/has* and the past participle of the verb. We form the past participle of regular verbs by adding *-ed* to the verb. The past participle of irregular verbs is different.

- We use the present perfect to talk about an action that started in the past and continues up to the present. When an action started in the past and ended in the past, we use the simple past. (See Unit 9.)

- We often use the present perfect with *for* and *since*. We use *for* to talk about length of time. We use *since* to talk about when a period of time began.

- *Have* is contracted to *'ve* in the positive and *haven't* in the negative. *Has* is contracted to *'s* in the positive and *hasn't* in the negative. We do not use contractions in affirmative short answers.

A. *Circle the correct word to complete each sentence.*

1. I've been a member of the Red Cross (for / since) 2008.
2. I (went / have been) to Sweden in 2009.
3. I've wanted to be a chemist (since / for) I was twelve.
4. The committee (gave / has given) the Nobel Peace Prize in Norway since 1901.
5. My friend (went / has gone) to the ceremony last year.
6. He's waited (for / since) ten years.

B. *Work with a partner. Talk about yourself. Then find out about your partner and share what you learn with the class. Use the present perfect.*

EXAMPLE: I came to this school in January 2010. I've been here since _____. I've been here for _____.

 PRONUNCIATION

HAVE/HAS AND FOR

A. *Listen to the sentences. Notice the weak stress of* have, has, *and* for. *Underline the stressed words.*

1. I have been here for three months.
2. She has been at this school for nine months.
3. We have been in this class for a year.
4. We have studied English for three years.
5. You have been in this city for ten years.
6. They have been here for ten days.

B. *Listen to the sentences again and repeat.*

CONVERSATION

A. *Listen to the conversation. Then listen again and repeat.*

Robin: Did you hear that the school has decided not to give a prize to the top student this year?

Julian: I know. <u>It comes as no surprise</u> that some students aren't happy about it.

Robin: My friend Jodie was very upset. She's worked very hard all year <u>in order to</u> win that prize. But maybe the school is right.

Julian: Maybe. I know that <u>in some cases</u> it makes the students compete instead of work together.

Do you know these expressions? What do you think they mean?

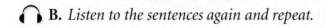

It comes as no surprise   in order to   in some cases

B. *Work with a partner. Practice a part of the conversation. Replace the underlined words with the words below.*

Robin: Did you hear that the school has decided not to give a prize to the top student this year?

Julian: I know. <u>It comes as no surprise that</u> some students are not happy about it.

As expected,   Understandably,

C. Your Turn. *Write a new conversation. Use some of the words below and your own ideas. Practice the conversation with a partner.*

It comes as no surprise   in order to   in some cases

 Go to page 157 for the Internet Activity.

| **DID YOU KNOW?** | • Mahatma Gandhi, an Indian man who worked tirelessly for peace and justice, never received the Nobel Peace Prize.
• Forty women and 773 men have received Nobel Peace Prizes. A few of them have received the prize more than once.
• They give the Nobel Peace Prize on December 10th each year, the anniversary of Alfred Nobel's death, in the presence of the King of Norway. |  |

A. COMPREHENSION

Circle the letter of the correct answer.

11. Paul Newman _____.

   a. mostly gave food to friends and family who needed help

   b. built a special camp for people who like to cook

   c. used his profits from Newman's Own to become a successful actor

   d. gave his money from acting and Newman's Own to charity

12. Deserts _____.

   a. are all very similar around the world

   b. have little plant and animal life

   c. are different in many ways, but they are all dry

   d. all have extreme heat and extreme cold

13. Some houses in the United States _____.

   a. are unique because of their shape

   b. have many different uses

   c. don't have roofs

   d. have no front or back doors

14. Saris _____.

   a. are not popular in all areas of India

   b. are two pieces of cloth

   c. are practical but not very stylish

   d. are one piece of cloth

15. Man-made islands _____.

   a. have different shapes, sizes, and materials they are made from

   b. are mostly places where rich people live

   c. are in only a few places in the world

   d. are not very strong

16. Cricket is _____.

    a. a sport similar to football that people play around the world

    b. a sport similar to baseball that is popular in countries that were once under British control

    c. a sport in which people throw a ball from one side of a field to another for many hours

    d. a sport that is only popular in a few countries in Asia and Africa

17. Australia is _____.

    a. a small tropical island with beautiful beaches

    b. a large country with different types of areas, plants, and animals

    c. a country with mostly hot, isolated areas where few people live

    d. a country with many people, large cities, and few natural areas

18. A national emblem is _____.

    a. a legend that tells the history of a country and its people

    b. a flag with colors and pictures that tell a story

    c. an animal or bird that symbolizes what the people of a country respect and admire

    d. a powerful animal or bird that lives only in a certain country

19. The ancient Greeks _____.

    a. had military leaders who killed anyone who did not support them

    b. had no religion and were great architects and builders

    c. believed in good health, a strong army, and a government by the people

    d. gave equal rights to men and women in all areas of their society

20. The purpose of the Nobel Peace Prize is to _____.

    a. help people make great inventions

    b. reward people who work to help others

    c. give money to the greatest people in medicine and science

    d. support the most powerful world leaders

B. VOCABULARY

Circle the letter of the correct answer.

11. The money or advantages you gain when you sell something are the _____.

    a. profits   **b.** philanthropy   **c.** success   **d.** collectors

12. Our _____ is the people, plants, and animals that are around us.

    a. charity   **b.** environment   **c.** kindness   **d.** region

13. Something strange is _____.

    a. spectacular   **b.** endangered   **c.** peculiar   **d.** grand

14. When things change or become different, they _____ what they were before.

    a. look like   **b.** depend on   **c.** forget about   **d.** vary from

15. When something is on top of the water and the water holds it up, it _____.

    a. floats   **b.** drops   **c.** melts   **d.** matches

16. The person who controls a game so that the players play by the rules is the _____.

    a. committee   **b.** coach   **c.** umpire   **d.** team

17. When the level of water in the sea is at its lowest during twenty-four hours, it is _____.

    a. low tide   **b.** off the coast   **c.** in season   **d.** below freezing

18. When a person is not afraid when in danger, he or she has _____.

    a. doubt   **b.** courage   **c.** privacy   **d.** respect

19. When something happens somewhere, it _____ there.

    a. makes laws   **b.** comes from   **c.** depends on   **d.** takes place

20. A person writes their wishes in a _____ about who to leave their property to after he or she dies.

    a. charity   **b.** will   **c.** camp   **d.** wrap

C. LANGUAGE FOCUS

Circle the letter of the correct answer.

11. John is _____ man I know.
    a. the succesfulest
    b. the most successful
    c. the most successfulest
    d. most successful

12. What _____ in the desert tonight?
    a. 'll the temperature be
    b. 'll the temperature
    c. going to be the temperature
    d. 's going the temperature

13. He _____ a small house to a big house.
    a. prefer
    b. preferring
    c. prefers
    d. is preferring

14. My aunt made _____ last year.
    a. to me a dress
    b. for me a dress
    c. a dress to me
    d. a dress for me

15. There _____ outside.
    a. isn't anyone
    b. is anyone
    c. isn't someone
    d. not anyone

16. This game is _____ soccer.

    a. as not exciting as

    b. not as exciting as

    c. as exciting not as

    d. as exciting

17. If he goes to Australia, he _____ with his sister in Sydney.

    a. stay

    b. stays

    c. 'll stay

    d. staying

18. Plants _____ sun to grow. Without it, they will die.

    a. must have

    b. must

    c. have to

    d. have

19. Where _____ to run?

    a. she train

    b. did she train

    c. she trained

    d. trained she

20. He _____ a member of the Red Cross since 2008.

    a. was

    b. been

    c. have been

    d. has been

APPENDICES

INTERNET ACTIVITIES

UNIT 1

Work in a small group. Use the Internet to find information about J.R.R. Tolkien, the author of the trilogy, or set of three books, The Lord of the Rings. *Answer the questions. Share your information with your classmates.*

1. Where and when was J.R.R. Tolkien born?
2. In what country did he live most of his life?
3. When did Tolkien write *The Lord of the Rings*?
4. In general, what is *The Lord of the Rings* about?
5. What other books did Tolkien write? (Name two.)

UNIT 2

Work in a small group. Use the Internet to find information on New Year's customs around the world. Choose one country from the list and answer the questions. Share your information with your classmates.

Belgium	Egypt	Germany	Thailand
China	Ethiopia	Iran	Vietnam

1. How do the people of this country celebrate the New Year?
2. Do they have special customs, eat special foods, or wear special clothing?
3. What is the meaning of each custom?

UNIT 3

Work in a small group. Use the Internet to find out about the White House (where the president of the United States lives). Answer the questions. Share your information with your classmates.

1. Where is the White House?
2. When was it built?
3. How many floors does the White House have?
4. Where do the President and his family live?
5. Where does the President work?
6. Where does the First Lady have her office?
7. What is the President's official schedule for one day? Choose the day you want.

UNIT 4

Work in a small group. Use the Internet to find two animals that are sacred in the following countries or cultures: ancient Egypt, Japan, China, Bali, Native Americans. Share your information with your classmates.

COUNTRY/CULTURE	SACRED ANIMALS
ANCIENT EGYPT	1.
	2.
JAPAN	1.
	2.
CHINA	1.
	2.
BALI	1.
	2.
NATIVE AMERICANS	1.
	2.

UNIT 5

Work in a small group. Use the Internet to learn more about wedding gift-giving customs around the world. Answer the questions. Share your information with your classmates.

1. What does a groom in Sudan give to the bride's family? Why?
2. What does a groom in Fiji present to the bride's father?
3. In China, what does the groom's family give to the bride's family on the day they are betrothed?
4. What is "bride price" in India? Why is it controversial today?
5. What does a groom give his bride in the Philippines?

UNIT 6

Work in a small group. Use the Internet to learn more about fugu—a typical food in Japan. Answer the questions. Share your information with your classmates.

1. What is fugu?
2. What does it look like?
3. What is dangerous about fugu?
4. Who can prepare fugu?
5. Which website gave you the best information? Which had the best pictures?

UNIT 7

Work in a small group. Use the Internet to learn about the Sami people of Norway. Focus either on the Sea Sami or the Mountain Sami. Answer the questions. Share your information with your classmates.

1. Who are the Sami?
2. Where do they live?
3. What is the geography and climate of these places?
4. What did traditional Sami houses look like?
5. What do their houses look like now?
6. What kinds of work do the Sami do?
7. What is their traditional clothing made from?
8. What do they eat and drink?
9. How do they travel?

UNIT 8

Work in a small group. Use the Internet to learn about plant life in oceans. Answer the questions. Share your information with your classmates.

1. Why are ocean plants important? Give two reasons.
2. Why are coral reefs particularly important? Give two reasons.
3. How does human pollution affect ocean plants and other sea life?
4. Which websites gave you the most information?

UNIT 9

Work in a small group. Look at the list of great monuments or "wonders" of the world. Use the Internet to research ONE of them. Answer the questions. Share your information with your classmates.

Angkor Wat	the Great Pyramid of Giza	Stonehenge
Chichen Itza	the Parthenon	the Taj Mahal

1. When and where was it built?
2. Who built it?
3. What is it? (Give a short description.)

UNIT 10

Work in a small group. Use the Internet to find a survival story (a story of someone who lived through a dangerous storm or natural disaster like a tornado, earthquake, tsunami, flood, etc.). Share your story with your classmates.

UNIT 11

Work in a small group. Look at the list of wealthy people, past and present. Use the Internet to research ONE of them. Answer the questions. Share your information with your classmates.

Bill Gates	Li Ka-shing	John D. Rockefeller
Hetty Green	Aristotle Onassis	Oprah Winfrey

1. When was he or she born?
2. Where did he or she live? OR Where does he or she live?
3. How did he or she get rich?
4. What did he or she do with his or her money? OR What does he or she do with his or her money?

UNIT 12

Work in a small group. Look at the list of places where living conditions are harsh. Use the Internet to research ONE of them. Answer the questions. Share your information with your classmates.

the Amazon rainforest	the Gobi Desert	the Sahara Desert
Death Valley	the North Pole	Siberia

1. Where is it located?
2. What is the weather like?
3. What are the highest and lowest temperatures there?
4. What does the place look like?
5. Why is it difficult to live there?

UNIT 13

Work in a small group. Look at the list of some unusual houses and buildings. Use the Internet to research ONE of them. Answer the questions. Share your information with your classmates.

the Basket Building	the Crooked House	the Kettle House
the Bubble House	the Dancing House	the Mushroom House
the Crazy House	the Football House	the Thin House

1. Where is it located?
2. When was it built?
3. Who built it?

UNIT 14

Work in a small group. Look at the list of some indigenous peoples from around the world. Use the Internet to research the traditional clothing of ONE of them. Find pictures of men and women in their traditional clothing and answer the questions. Share the pictures and your information with your classmates.

the Navajo (United States)	the Mapuche (Chile)	the Inuit (Alaska)
the Zulu (South Africa)	the Hmong (China)	the Kuna (Panama)

1. What does the clothing look like?
2. What do women wear? What do men wear?
3. How do they make the clothing?
4. Which website had the best information? Which had the best pictures?

UNIT 15

Work in a small group. Use the Internet to learn about The Great Pacific Garbage Patch, sometimes referred to as "Garbage Island." Share your information with your classmates.

1. Where is Garbage Island located?
2. What is Garbage Island made up of?
3. How was it formed?
4. What effect does Garbage Island have on wildlife?
5. What can humans do to help fight the problem?

UNIT 16

Work in a small group. Look at the list of sports. Use the Internet to research ONE of them. Find out where, when, and how it began. Share your information with your classmates.

basketball	curling	golf	rugby
camel racing	dog sledding	polo	skiing

UNIT 17

Work in a small group. Imagine that you have five days to visit Australia. Use the Internet to find a travel guide to Australia. Write a travel schedule that tells where you want to go and what you want to do and see in those five days. You can see and do more than one thing in a day. Share your schedule with your classmates.

Day 1	Day 2	Day 3	Day 4	Day 5
• Visit the Sydney Opera House				

UNIT 18 •

Work in a small group. Look at the list of animals commonly used as emblems. Use the Internet to research ONE of them. Answer the questions. Share your information with your classmates.

condor	eagle	lion	tiger	wolf

1. What country or countries use the animal on their national emblem?
2. What does the animal symbolize?

UNIT 19 •

Work in a small group. Use the Internet to learn more about the ancient Greeks. Answer the questions. Share your information with your classmates.

1. In what time period did the ancient Greeks live?
2. What kinds of clothes did the ancient Greeks wear?
3. What kind of houses did they live in?
4. What did they make their houses from?
5. What kinds of weapons did they have?
6. What did the ancient Greeks give to the world?
7. Which website gave you the best information? Which had the best pictures?

UNIT 20 •

Work in a small group. Look at the list of Nobel Peace Prize winners. Use the Internet to research ONE of them. Answer the questions. Share your information with your classmates.

Aung San Suu Kyi	Barack Obama	Rigoberta Menchú
Wangari Maathai	Kofi Annan	Amnesty International

1. Who are they?
2. Why did they win the Nobel Peace Prize?
3. Do you think they deserved to win?

MAP OF THE WORLD

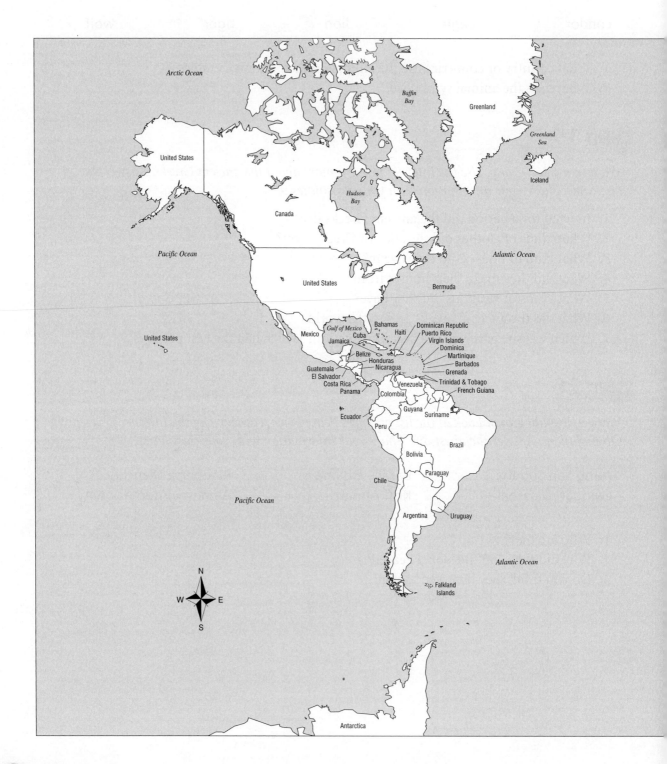

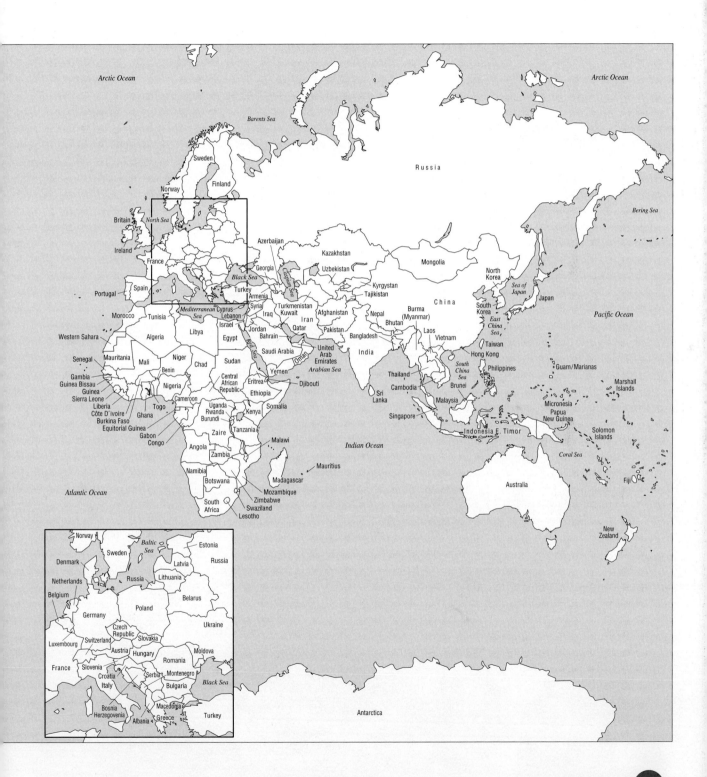

Arctic Ocean

Barents Sea

Sweden

Finland

Norway

Britain

North Sea

Ireland

France

Portugal

Spain

Morocco

Tunisia

Mediterranean Sea

Cyprus

Lebanon

Israel

Western Sahara

Algeria

Libya

Egypt

Senegal

Mauritania

Mali

Niger

Chad

Gambia

Benin

Guinea Bissau

Guinea

Nigeria

Sierra Leone

Liberia

Côte D'ivoire

Ghana

Togo

Burkina Faso

Cameroon

Equitorial Guinea

Gabon

Congo

Uganda

Rwanda

Burundi

Central African Republic

Sudan

Eritrea

Ethiopia

Kenya

Somalia

Tanzania

Zaire

Malawi

Angola

Zambia

Djibouti

Yemen

Red Sea

Saudi Arabia

Oman

United Arab Emirates

Arabian Sea

Qatar

Bahrain

Jordan

Iraq

Syria

Armenia

Azerbaijan

Georgia

Black Sea

Turkey

Caspian Sea

Kazakhstan

Uzbekistan

Turkmenistan

Kuwait

Iran

Pakistan

Afghanistan

Kyrgystan

Tajikistan

Nepal

Bhutan

India

Bangladesh

Burma (Myanmar)

Mongolia

China

North Korea

Sea of Japan

South Korea

Japan

East China Sea

Laos

Vietnam

Taiwan

Hong Kong

Thailand

Cambodia

South China Sea

Brunei

Malaysia

Singapore

Sri Lanka

Indonesia

E. Timor

Philippines

Guam/Marianas

Marshall Islands

Micronesia

Papua New Guinea

Solomon Islands

Fiji

Coral Sea

Australia

New Zealand

Namibia

Botswana

Madagascar

Mauritius

Zimbabwe

Mozambique

South Africa

Swaziland

Lesotho

Atlantic Ocean

Indian Ocean

Pacific Ocean

Arctic Ocean

Bering Sea

Russia

Antarctica

Norway

Baltic Sea

Sweden

Denmark

Estonia

Latvia

Russia

Netherlands

Russia

Lithuania

Belgium

Belarus

Germany

Poland

Luxembourg

Czech Republic

Slovakia

Ukraine

Switzerland

Austria

Hungary

Moldova

France

Slovenia

Romania

Croatia

Serbia

Montenegro

Italy

Bulgaria

Black Sea

Bosnia Herzegovenia

Macedonia

Albania

Greece

Turkey